VIOLENCE!

VIOLENCE!

OUR FASTEST-GROWING PUBLIC HEALTH PROBLEM

BY

John Langone

Little, Brown and Company
BOSTON   TORONTO

Fourth Printing

Library of Congress Cataloging in Publication Data

Langone, John, 1929–
    Violence! : our fastest-growing public health
problem.

    Includes bibliographical references and index.
    Summary: Examines the roots and outward manifesta-
tions of aggression and violence, the role of society and
the individual, and what can be done to lessen the trend
toward violent behavior and encourage a peaceful
approach.
    1. Violence—Juvenile literature.   2. Aggressiveness
(Psychology)—Juvenile literature.   3. Violent crimes—
Juvenile literature.   4. Violence—Prevention—
Juvenile literature.   [1. Violence.   2. Aggressiveness
(Psychology)]   I. Title
HM291.L255   1984   303.6'2   84-5674
ISBN 0-316-51431-4

BP

*Published simultaneously in Canada
by Little, Brown & Company (Canada) Limited*

PRINTED IN THE UNITED STATES OF AMERICA

To Dale Meyn, with affection

CONTENTS

VIOLENCE!

INTRODUCTION

Violence is necessary; it is as American as cherry pie.

— BLACK MILITANT H. RAP BROWN,
in a 1966 remark

VIOLENT BEHAVIOR, the application of great physical force to damage or destroy, has been with us from the dawn of history, and it is not only an American problem. Before there were newspapers or radio or television to alert us to its presence, before there were any police and prisons to protect us from those who practiced it, violence existed. We know from the Bible that Cain, the firstborn son of Adam and Eve, committed the first recorded murder when he killed his brother, Abel, in a fit of jealousy, and was cursed by God, who set a mark upon him for it. Anthropologists can tell us, from the ancient evidence of human skulls shattered by hand axes, that primitive man destroyed his enemies and his rivals; we do not know his reasons, but chances are he did it to protect himself or his property, or out of rage, or because of some uncontrollable impulse he could not understand.

Human beings have also long used violence to extract confessions of guilt, or to get information, or simply to punish, and some of the torturer's medieval tools are generally well known to us all: thumbscrews to crush the bones, the rack to stretch the arms and legs and pull limbs out of their sockets, the box-shaped Iron Maiden, whose spiked interior meant a slow death for those unfortunate enough to be forced inside. We know, too, that ritual violence existed — and still does exist — among tribesmen in faraway places and among our more "civilized" neighbors. We read of tribesmen who mark the coming of age of young boys and girls by flogging and mutilation, their bodies stung by wasps, or pepper rubbed into wounds created by coats of thorns; of cannibals who eat the flesh and drink the blood of their enemies in order to destroy the enemy tribe's power; of scalps taken by Indians from our own northern plains, of heads taken by their counterparts in South America; of human sacrifices by the ancient Aztecs; of ritual murders in fashionable apartments in our largest cities by self-styled witches and warlocks; of ritual violence by deluded cult followers.

The violence we read about today is not really all that different from that of the past. Neither is it peculiar to one generation or another; every generation believes that the successive generation is more troubled, wilder, more violent than its own. The truth is, your grandparents' generation worried about your parents; and your great-grandparents undoubtedly worried about your grandparents. So long as human beings hate and love, are greedy and jealous, hungry, poor, and insane, or seek power, they will strike out to injure one another, either physically or emotionally, or even to kill.

True, the weapons used to do this may be modern — automatic rifles, submachine guns, bombs so tiny they can be slipped into an envelope and mailed to a victim — but their function, and the reasons for their use, are exactly the same as for the Australian aborigine's boomerang, the Brazilian Indian's blowgun and poisoned darts, the Fiji native's spear edged with shark teeth, the American Indian's tomahawk, the slingshot David used to slay Goliath. Modern-day torturers, too, are not much different from the hooded monsters who did their work in castle dungeons — except that instead of the rack or the Iron Maiden, they may now employ electric shock, or a more sophisticated form of mental violence popularly known as brainwashing, along with the standard methods of inflicting pain. It can truly be said that where there is a will to commit violence, there is, indeed, a way. And make no mistake about it, the will is there. In one recent, bloody weekend alone, in New York City, fifteen people, including a twenty-three-month-old baby, were slain; one of the victims was murdered during a holdup that netted the gunmen just fifty dollars. "In an environment of violence, life becomes not only tentative but cheap," writer and editor Norman Cousins has observed. "The sense of beauty, the capacity to be awakened and enlarged by a tender experience, the possibilities of compassionate thought — all these are being crowded and pressured by the language of force. The mind of man is rapidly being hammered out of shape by the constant pounding of explosive accusations, denunciations, and vilifications . all tied to the casual and precipitate use of force. Nothing multiplies more easily than force. Whatever man's other shortages — food, learning and work — he has no shortage of devices or instruments for expressing his raw anger. Guns have a way of materializing more readily than the commodities that sustain life or the undertakings that dignify or enlarge it."[1]

The force of which Cousins speaks so eloquently is, indeed, so commonplace that a mugging, an underworld murder, a hostage-taking, a student riot, a rape, an incident of child abuse, even a political assassination, often causes hardly a stir when it is reported. Sometimes, too, we discuss each incident of violence as easily as we would the action on a baseball field or on a stage. Even the young have become quite knowledgeable about violence. Recently, the *New York Times* told of a group of New York City third-graders who had watched films of the assassination attempt on President Reagan on television — in slow motion, and many times. When questioned by a teacher whose purpose was to put the subject of violence into perspective, the youngsters showed they knew a good deal about the incident, even such things as the caliber of the gun used. Some of the remarks of the children: "It was one inch away from his heart." "It went into his lung and it collapsed. It hit a rib." "They didn't want to wait for an ambulance, so they took the limousine and let him walk in." "Reagan said to the doctor, 'Please tell me you're a Republican.' "[2]

There is little doubt that violence is, today, a public health problem of enormous proportions, one that has spread far beyond the city's "bad" neighborhoods to the "quiet" suburbs and the countryside. Crime statistics are one measure of the seriousness of the problem. While statistics vary from year to year, depending on national attitudes toward the criminal and punishment, on racial tension and the state of the economy, the following represent a general picture of the current crisis:

- Some 23,000 people are murdered in the United States each year — roughly 400 victims a week, or one every half hour. Most of the victims know their assailants because the attacks are usually the result of a family or neighborhood argument, gang wars, or drug-related quarrels. About a third of the victims are killed by total strangers, sometimes for no apparent reason.

- People younger than eighteen commit a quarter of the violent crimes, and are more likely than adults to do so in gangs of three or more. Moreover, the number of murders committed by young people between the ages of fifteen and twenty-four has more than doubled over the past twenty years. Most violent crimes are, in fact, committed by this age group.

- More than 80,000 forcible rapes occur in a year.

- Nearly 25 million households experience a crime of violence or theft in any given year.

- More than 100,000 teachers are physically assaulted every year by students.

- In the last fifteen years, at least 2 million people around the world have been executed without a proper trial.

It is no wonder, in light of such a disturbing litany, that people are so fearful of being targets of violence that 45 percent of them are afraid to go out alone at night within a mile of their homes. More and more homeowners and shopkeepers are arming themselves to protect their families and their property: in 1981, residents of Houston, Texas, shot and killed twenty-five criminal suspects; in New York City, fifteen such killings were reported. "The fear of violent crime is a pervasive influence in American life," says a recent study of fearful Americans. "Among the particularly fearful are people who live in large cities, the young, women, blacks, and those with higher levels of formal education."[3]

In the pages ahead, we will look at some specific categories and instances of violence, and try to answer some of the deeply troubling questions that violent behavior raises. Why, for example, do people become aggressive? Why do they kill? Is it a result of something coded in their genes, like the color of hair and eyes? Is it because of a damaged brain? Or, if the tendency toward violence is not handed down through our ancestors or caused by an injury, such as a blow to the head, is it learned behavior, an aberration we can blame on our environment, or the bad example of others? Do our racial origins, our cultural heritage, where we live, television, movies, or the climate have anything to do with violence? Why are public figures like President John F. Kennedy and Beatle John Lennon assassinated? Can anything be done about violence? Is stern punishment the answer? Stricter police control? Gun control? More prisons? Or does the cure lie, as former FBI Director J. Edgar Hoover once suggested, "not in the electric chair but the high chair"?

While moral considerations are obviously important in such a discussion, they are not part of this book. Neither are questions of war, perhaps the most glaring example of violence, nor the systematic slaughter of a race, such as the Nazi extermination of the Jews. These topics were covered in detail in a previous book for young readers by this author, *Thorny Issues*.

My purpose is not to judge violent acts beyond the implicit message that they offend human dignity, nor to influence the reader to judge them; rather, it is to provide some insight into why people behave violently, and perhaps some clues as to what may be done to prevent such behavior. Many myths and misconceptions are associated with violence, and it is hoped that some of these will be dispelled, and that my young readers will then have a clearer understanding of the complex mix of biological, sociological, and psychological factors that lie at the root of aggressive behavior.

· 1 ·

THE CAUSES OF
VIOLENCE

*Is there any cause in nature that makes
these hard hearts?*

— SHAKESPEARE

WE HAVE DEFINED VIOLENCE as the use of physical force
to abuse, injure, or kill. But the definition does not tell
us why human beings harm one another. Are we born
violent? That is, do we carry genes inherited from animal ancestors with vicious instincts? Do we learn such
behavior from parents and playmates, from movies and
television, from books? Can a blow on the head, a brain
injury caused by a virus, or being drunk make one violent?

There are very strong differences of opinion about
the roles these things play in violent behavior. Scientists
know what lies behind the fury of a tornado, the eruption of a volcano, and the explosion of a hydrogen
bomb — all examples of another kind of violence. But
they are still not able to agree about what causes human
violence. The disagreement is part of the time-honored

nature-versus-nurture debate — *nature* meaning the genes that we inherit from our parents, *nurture* meaning our social and economic status, where we live, where we work; nurture involves all of the outside influences in our lives.

Over the years, one or the other of the two major theories becomes fashionable and accepted; which one usually depends on the status and influence of different scientists and writers, on dramatic new laboratory research, even on an outbreak of a large number of strikingly similar acts of violence that seems to prove one of the theories.

It is, however, a mistake to take any one of the arguments and lean on it as the prime reason people behave violently. We are, after all, the products of both heredity and environment, nature and nurture, intertwined. To exclude one or the other is not appropriate when dealing with an organism as complex as a human being — despite the ease with which people liken us to machines, and our brains to computers. We are infinitely more complicated than such human-made objects, and so are our actions. If we select heredity over environment, or vice versa, when discussing violent behavior, the choice forces us to believe that everyone will, for example, kill or become aggressive under a given set of circumstances. If that were so, everyone living in a poor or "bad" neighborhood would turn out wrong; anyone whose father or grandmother was a murderer would be at risk of inheriting a murderer's genes. None of this is true. People commit crimes for many reasons, and we should remember that honest, hard-working, and nonaggressive people come out of poverty; and that no one has yet isolated a gene that codes for crime.

The only sensible approach is to play it safe — that is, to appreciate the complexity of the mixture of the biological, sociological, and psychological factors that go into molding the person who becomes violent.

It is probably true, on the other hand, that we all inherit the *potential* to behave violently; but we do not inherit the violent behavior *itself.* Proof of this may be seen in the fact that many people and animals who have committed a violent act can live for many years, or for the rest of their lives, without doing so again. By the same token, people who have never become abusive may become so suddenly when something or someone irritates them or provokes them.

Another way to explain the difference between our potential to act violently and the actual commission of a violent act is to say that biology and our genetic inheritance constitute a firecracker and its fuse, a tightly rolled package of powder that *can* explode. The powder is made up of a number of ingredients: hormones, powerful chemicals that originate in our glands and circulate through our bodies to regulate various functions, as well as our very moods; brain chemicals that transmit electrical signals, directing the way we think and feel and act; defective or extra chromosomes, errors in the threadlike bits of genetic material that are responsible for numerous mental aberrations from schizophrenia to retardation to aggressive behavior.

To set it all off, we need a match, or some form of

heat. In this case, our "match" is another complicated mix that includes all of the things that go into our environment — our living conditions, our friends, how much money we make, all sorts of situations and circumstances. But merely applying a match to a firecracker fuse does not guarantee an explosion. For one thing, the powder may not be all that powerful; it may lack the necessary proportion of key ingredients to ignite it. The match, too, may burn out before it can be applied to the fuse — in our analogy, this might mean that the circumstances that can ignite the powder may lessen, or disappear completely. And to carry our example a step farther, the fuse itself — which we can liken to the impulse-control system that keeps most of us from behaving badly all the time — may be too damp to carry the spark.

We should be able to see, then, that violent actions cannot be explained simply by drawing attention to single causes. The conditions must be just right before one behaves violently.

Before we look at some of the conditions and ingredients that can lead to violence, some definitions are in order. Although the terms *aggression* and *violence* are sometimes used to mean different things — a person who is aggressive in business or in pursuing knowledge, for instance, may not demonstrate violent tendencies at all — they will be used interchangeably for our purposes. Psychologists define aggression as violent, angry, hostile, and destructive behavior. Sometimes it is turned against objects as well as people, as when a vandal overturns gravestones or sprays graffiti over public walls and streets. Other times, it is turned inward, as when a person commits suicide.

Although some cultural groups and some animals show little or no aggression, it is generally true that aggressive behavior can be found virtually everywhere — among fish, and insects, as well as among humans, and animals. We all know that dogs and cats fight, that blue jays attack squirrels, that ants make war. Sometimes, animals attack one another for food, to protect their territory against intruders, or to establish their positions as leaders in a group; at other times, the reasons are unclear. In a recent report from the Oregon Regional Primate Research Center, scientists told of behavior among groups of rhesus monkeys that had been imported from India. In one outbreak of severe fighting, twelve adult female monkeys were killed. "The cause of this aggression was not clear," said the scientists. "Although human beings generally consider killing members of one's own species reprehensible, there are many well-documented cases of animals in natural settings killing their own kind. For example, male langur monkeys sometimes invade a troop, drive out the resident male, and then kill young infants; roving bands of male chimpanzees enter neighboring communities and beat other adult male chimpanzees to death; nomadic male lions kill strange cubs; male elephant seals crush and females bite to death young pups in breeding rookeries; male mountain sheep kill [males of the same species] in fights over access to females; and young eagles push siblings out of the nest to their deaths."[1]

The scientists presented such examples, not to argue that the deaths among their monkeys were natural occurrences, but to emphasize that competitive, lethally aggressive behavior is common in many species, and that the magnitude of the aggression among the monkeys was unusual, not the fact that animals were killed.

Honeybees, too, those buzzing creatures responsible for bringing tasty treats to our tables, can be mean. One aggressive strain of African bees that spread recently across South America and then headed north is easily angered, and has reportedly made unprovoked attacks on people and livestock. Writer Annie Dillard, in her memorable book *Pilgrim at Tinker Creek,* had the following chilling observations to make about insects: "Fish gotta swim and bird gotta fly; insects, it seems, gotta do one horrible thing after another. I never ask why of a vulture or shark, but I ask why of almost every insect I see. More than one insect — the possibility of fertile reproduction — is an assault on all human value, all hope of a reasonable god. Even that devout Frenchman, J. Henri Fabre, who devoted his entire life to the study of insects, cannot restrain a feeling of unholy revulsion. He describes a bee-eating wasp, the Philanthus, who has killed a honeybee. If the bee is heavy with honey, the wasp squeezes its crop 'so as to disgorge the delicious syrup, which she drinks by licking the tongue which her unfortunate victim, in her death-agony, sticks out of her mouth at full length. . . . At the moment of some such horrible banquet, I have seen the Wasp, with her prey, seized by the Mantis: the bandit was rifled by another bandit. And here is the awful detail: while the Mantis held her transfixed under the points of the double saw and was already munching her belly, the Wasp continued to lick the honey of her Bee, unable to relinquish the delicious food even amid the terrors of death.' "[2]

Such examples drawn from the behavior of nonhuman creatures demonstrate that they, too, are capable of doing awful things to one another. But beyond that, one should not draw too many analogies between them and us. While mice have been called "miniature humans" by scientists, and much has been learned about treating human disease from them, the fact remains that we can reason, and animals cannot. Thus, any inferences drawn from animal aggression should not be too readily applied to humans; while their actions may be directed by instinct, this is not to say that all of ours are also. Nonetheless, several prominent scientists and writers have suggested that because we evolved from animals with violent instincts we, too, carry such impulses about in us like time bombs. Human beings, they say, are natural predators who require violence for nourishment. As writer Robert Ardrey has put it, "We enjoy the violent. We hurry to an accident not to help, we run to a fire not to put it out, we crowd about a schoolyard fight not to stop it."[3]

Many of those who believe that aggression can be traced to internal sources say that certain acts of aggression are often a way of discharging energy that, if pent up, might burst out in an explosion of more serious violence, or result in suicide. Some people, it is believed, release their aggressions by turning against an inanimate object, by watching a violent sport, by participating in such a sport — or even by forcefully pursuing some difficult goal.

The great Austrian neurologist Sigmund Freud (1856–1939) was one who believed that a single aggressive drive was behind a wide range of aggressive and nonaggressive actions. One of his lines of reasoning went this way: Since the dominant tendency in all organic life is to reduce nervous tension, all life forms seek death in order to be free. But because the death instinct, called *Thanatos,* is opposed by the life instinct, *Eros,* the destructive drive is diverted from the self to others. Therefore, by attacking others, a person finds release from the pressures that ordinarily would cause him or her to seek death.

Freud's theories, of course, influenced many psychiatrists, and they were also responsible for many opposing schools of thought. His concept of the death instinct in connection with aggression is an example of one much-debated theory. As one treatise observes, "Empirical evidence provides little support for Freud's analysis of aggressive behavior. To cite just one difficulty, research clearly indicates that organisms do not seek the complete elimination of excitation. There are many situations in which human beings as well as lower animals work for an increase in stimulation. Death is not necessarily the inherent aim of all organic life."[4] Moreover, Freud's critics point out, even though our body's cells die regularly, it does not necessarily follow that this is an inborn goal of the whole body.

Another proponent of the view that aggressiveness is innate in all living things, that it can be explained in terms of some inner fire or force, is Konrad Lorenz, the eminent Austrian-born specialist in animal behavior. He has described aggression as "the fighting instinct in beast and man" that is directed against members of the same species. He adds flatly, "There cannot be any doubt, in the opinion of any biologically minded scientist, that intraspecific aggression is, in man, just as much of a spontaneous instinctive drive as in most other higher vertebrates."[5]

But this view, too, has come under fire. Jeffrey H. Goldstein, a Temple University social psychologist, found two difficulties with Lorenz's statement. "First, the evidence that animals, at least the higher primates, are instinctively aggressive is not at all convincing. . . . Second, even if the evidence . . . were sufficient to warrant the conclusion that infrahuman [less or lower than human] species were innately violent, we would still have to ask whether that proves anything at all about proneness to aggression in man. The answer, of course, is that it does not. The *likelihood* that man is instinctively aggressive would be increased if all animals were shown conclusively to be aggressive, but we would still have to entertain the possibility that Homo sapiens, having evolved as an independent species, was not."[6]

Goldstein argues that there is little doubt that man *can* behave like inferior species. But, he says, it is wrong to say that because man can do so, this is the way he *must* behave. Animals, after all, are animals, despite the human attributes we and Walt Disney enjoy imagining they possess. It may well be, then, that what causes them to be aggressive is not always the same as what causes us to be so. Perhaps the words of the English historian James Anthony Froude tell us something: "Wild animals never kill for sport.   Man is the only one to whom the torture and death of his fellow creatures is amusing in itself." In light of such an astute statement, one has to wonder if man is, as the poets like to say, truly a noble animal.

We human beings do, of course, have instincts — call them inherited memories — that make us act without reasoning. The desire for food and sex are among them. But though we do act with fear and hostility toward people who threaten us, the proof that we have inborn reasons for doing so is sorely lacking. Geneticists sometimes cite cases in which an achieving father or mother produces an outstanding child — a brilliant scientist may have an equally brilliant scientist son or daughter — as examples of the power of heredity. But is that the reason a child becomes a star student? Is a composer talented because his father was a celebrated concertmaster? Despite the argument that such special talent is imprinted in the genes, no one is sure whether it is that or the environment in which a child is raised that influences him or her. Writes Dr. Lynn Gillis, professor of psychiatry at the University of Cape Town:

We see, therefore, that although we all have inborn urges in common and human nature is the same everywhere, both can be greatly modified by upbringing and are expressed in different ways in different cultures. There can be no doubt, for example, that people everywhere are susceptible to aggressive feelings. In some warlike tribes or nations, these may be legitimately channelled off during periodic outbreaks of war or fighting. Such people glorify war and praise deeds of valour and destruction. In other more peace-loving cultures, the direct expression of aggression is frowned upon and wars seldom take place. These differences of behaviour reflect the differences between the systems of values maintained in the various cultures and instilled in their members particularly during early childhood training: one people will teach its young that it is right to stand up and fight, and another that it is wiser to run away; and the interesting fact is that a child born within the first group but brought up within the second, will take on all the qualities of those he has lived among apart from physical characteristics which can never be changed, such as the colour of the skin. For this reason, it is never wise to ascribe too much in the way of motivation to inborn factors, for motives are due, in most cases, rather to nurture than to nature. Of course, we have a natural tendency to blame our failures or deficiencies upon what we firmly believe was born with us — "It is just my nature," we say, or "I cannot help it, I was born like that." More often than not, these are merely excuses and impede us from gaining further psychological knowledge of our real selves.[7]

The strong belief that aggression is a learned rather than an inherited response is supported by a number of observations and experiments in both animals and humans. More than fifty years ago, experiments with cats and rats showed that when these animals, thought to be instinctive enemies, are brought up together, they do not necessarily become hostile to one another when they are adults. The rats are not afraid of the cats, and the cats do not attack the rats, even when hungry. If the young cats are allowed to watch their mothers kill rats regularly, however, most of them will do the same when they grow up. And interestingly, they will kill only the species they have seen the mother kill. Moreover, it is not unusual to hear of instances of other animals' caring for infant animals of species that are supposedly their natural enemies.

With regard to human beings, studies of child abuse — a subject we will deal with separately later on — lend further support to the notion that violence is learned. It is known, for instance, that children who are deprived of love and are beaten will often become child beaters themselves when they become parents. Children may also learn the actual techniques of aggression from adults. In one study group, children were shown a film of an adult violently attacking a stuffed clown doll; they imitated the adults' behavior when they were left alone with the doll.

Learning is also important when we consider another strong response, love. Years ago, many people believed that love was instinctive behavior, that it just occurred naturally. And often it was confused with the sex drive, an instinct that comes with our biological heritage, one that has much to do with the desire to seek pleasure from members of the opposite sex. Sexual attraction, it is true, plays an important part in love. But love itself is not an instinct. Rather, we learn how to love, and we do that because of the various influences in our environment, in our culture. There is a good deal to be said for the importance of a loving environment at home when considering violence. It has been demonstrated time and again that a harsh atmosphere in the home, or a home with no caring parents, makes a young person ignorant of love and thus unable to love. When a child from such a background grows up, he or she may not be able to make lasting friends, or may become a domineering parent or a cruel parent. These children might even suffer from low self-esteem, feeling that they have no worth or are not good enough for anything or anyone. Moreover, if they have a desire to show love, they may not be able to express it because of a fear of being rejected. If love were stamped in our genes, if there were a gene that spelled it out — L-O-V-E — such people would probably not have the difficulties they do. They would simply be programmed to love. Yet, we know that this is not so.

It should be fairly obvious, then, that we need teachers to show us how to be kind — and how to be violent. Before a person breaks into a store, knocks someone unconscious with a club or fists, kills with a knife, or loads and fires a handgun, he or she has had to learn how to do those things. Such knowledge does not automatically spring into a person's head. It has to be acquired — by watching, by being told how, perhaps even by reading. Youth gangs, for example, learn to be violent from their leaders and from other members of the gang. They learn how to use a weapon, how to make one, where to aim a stunning blow to the body. Gang members also learn soon enough that deviant behavior is easier and sometimes more rewarding than conformist behavior. They learn that crime does, indeed, pay. They learn that as long as they do what the group does they will be rewarded with material goods, and with official membership in the group — the last being most important because it gives this sort of youth an identity he or she may not have had before. Gang members also learn that what they do gets them a lot of attention. Newspapers, radio, and television cover their activities fairly regularly, all of which tends to feed the gang's ego and to make its members even more aggressive. Dr. Jerome Stumphauzer, who developed a delinquency-prevention program at the Los Angeles County–University of Southern California Medical Center, once observed, "Many of these youths carry newspaper clippings of their gang's exploits in their wallets, or will cluster around a television set if a station announces a special on gang violence."[8]

A gang member's mother and father may also be partly responsible for the member's behavior. "Some parents are still involved in this lifestyle," said Dr. Stumphauzer. "They encourage their children to adopt it. We've seen a grandmother, mother and her daughter all bearing the same gang tattoo on their left hands as a reminder of the historical pervasiveness of this problem."[9]

That remark also does a bit more than simply point a finger at how gang membership may be reinforced at home. The mention of mother, grandmother, and daughter should dispel any notion you might have that it is only males who become criminals. There is no doubt that women have been less apt to engage in criminal activities than men. This has nothing to do with biological differences, but with different social upbringings and different cultural roles. A U.S. government report on crimes of violence puts the issue of female violence this way: "The female child is usually more supervised than the male; she is taught to be soft, gentle, and compliant, while, especially in the ghetto subculture, the male is encouraged to be tough. The woman's role as wife, mother, and homemaker tends to involve her in far fewer situations that can lead to criminal or violent behavior. Even if a woman is caught up in the meshes of the law, the social attitude toward her tends to be sympathetic and protective, rather than harsh and punitive. Importantly, however, when the cultural roles of women and men come to resemble each other, their rates of crime and violence also become more similar."[10]

That may well be. But, still, a look backward at history, a glance at the daily newspapers, an evening at the movies — all will tell you that the popular expression "weaker sex" is not always appropriate. Britain's Queen Mary I (1553–1558), known as "Bloody Mary," restored Catholicism to England, but she had nearly three hundred Protestants burned at the stake in doing so. Lady Macbeth never killed anyone directly, but she urged her husband to murder King Duncan, and rebuked Macbeth for wavering. In Greek mythology, Medea, a princess and sorceress, was especially bloodthirsty. She helped Jason of the Argonauts steal the Golden Fleece and murder her half brother. Later, after marrying Jason, she convinced two young women to cut their father, an enemy of Jason's, to pieces. Medea next murdered her two children by Jason, then tried to poison her second husband's son. Closer to home, there was Bonnie Parker of Bonnie and Clyde fame, murderous Ma Barker and her boys, and Carol Fugate, who in 1958, at the age of fourteen, went on a murder rampage through the Nebraska countryside with her boy-friend, Charlie Starkweather; eleven people died in the carnage, which became the theme of a movie, *Badlands,* and a song, "Nebraska," by Bruce Springsteen. More recently, there was the tale of Phoolan Devi, a twenty-seven-year-old bandit who ran wild over a state in India for four years, pursued by thousands of police. Phoolan was charged with seventy incidents of banditry, and suspected of fifty murders. She eventually surrendered.

Phoolan learned violence at an early age. A few months after she was married, at age eleven, she was beaten and thrown out of the house by her husband. Later, she was raped by policemen, and then by prisoners during the times she spent in jail. Not surprisingly, she fell in with a bandit chief, then formed her own gang.

Undoubtedly, it was this way of life, and Phoolan's companions, that led her astray. The same thing happens over and over in our own society when young people are introduced to crime and violence at an early age. But often it is society in general — a wastebasket term that means our neighborhoods, and the communities and families that make up society — that may be blamed for the wrong kind of teaching. We know, for example, that the slum areas of our large cities, those communities where it is difficult, if not impossible, to teach young people to respect the law, have the highest crime rates. Many people who live in such environments never commit a serious crime. But more than likely they have all been the victim of some assault, or know someone who has. Former U.S. Attorney General Ramsey

Clark has written graphically of the relationship between crime and deprived neighborhoods:

> Most crime in America is born in environments saturated in poverty and its consequences: illness, ignorance, idleness, ugly surroundings, hopelessness. Crime incubates in places where thousands have no jobs, and those who do have the poorest jobs; where houses are old, dirty and dangerous; where people have no rights ... Probably four in five of all serious crimes flow from places of extreme poverty and most are inflicted on the people who live there. ... It is well to be concerned about crime among affluent suburban teenagers, drugs in high schools and protests by college students. These are matters with which we must deal sensitively and effectively. To the segregated country club set, they encompass much of the direct experience with crime. But beyond this narrow life is the real world of crime and violence that is the overwhelming part of the whole. It is the poor, the slum dweller, the disadvantaged who suffer most, and most tragically, the crime of America. It is here that the clear connection between crime and the harvest of poverty — ignorance, disease, slums, discrimination, segregation, despair and injustice — is manifest.
>
> Every major city in America demonstrates the relationship between crime and poor education, unemployment, bad health, and inadequate housing. When we understand this, we take much of the mystery out of crime. We may prefer the mystery. If so, we are condemned to live with crime we could prevent.[11]

Such conditions that Clark speaks about injure what we can call one's self-concept — that is, how someone perceives himself or herself. When a person is alienated from society's mainstream, he or she cannot help feeling worthless. Some years ago, the U.S. Department of Health, Education and Welfare explored the self-concepts of delinquent persons. As we know, delinquency is closely related to such factors as broken homes, poverty, poor impulse control, and inadequate adult models. Some of what the agency found follows:

- The typical delinquent dislikes himself. He has a negative self-concept, especially in regard to his behavior, his moral self, and his family self.
- His self-concept shows many of the maladjustments that suggest personality disorder. He suffers from inner tension and discomfort, is very much at odds with himself, and this often throws him into conflict with society. He is also too unstable and immature to withstand stress and frustration. Troubled and deviant, he finds it very hard to cope with life. Seeing himself as bad and worthless, he acts accordingly.
- He has an uncertain picture of himself, and is easily influenced by external suggestion and by his environment. He tends to look outward for control and evaluation of his behavior.
- He often makes little effort to portray himself in a good light.
- Repeated criminal behavior reinforces and further lowers the already deviant and negative self-concept of the delinquent.

A bleak environment, as has been said, can do all of that to a person. And it is no wonder that many people who live in deprived neighborhoods have a warped sense of values that wipes away any respect or sympathy for others. They react violently, not only against those who intrude into their neighborhood, but against those who live there as well. It is simply not true that the only victims of violence in the ghetto are people who stray there. Among urban blacks, for instance, who have a crime rate far higher than that of urban whites, most of the victims are black. In the rough neighborhoods — or, as the song "Bad, Bad, Leroy Brown" put it, "in the baddest part of town" — there is little talk of whether something is right or wrong; for the ghetto resident, it is rather a question of what must be done to survive, and how to demonstrate one's authority. Murder is common in such places, and the victim is usually someone the murderer knows. Drugs are often at the root of murders that occur in ghetto areas. Said one detective in New York City, where a fourth of the homicides in 1981 were tied to drugs, "The use of drugs has become more extensive and pervasive, and when you have people selling drugs, you have guns, rivalries, rip-offs, and inevitably, violence."[12]

Alcohol, which is a drug, also plays a part in the violence, though in a different way. It is legal, thus there is no connection between selling alcohol and violence — although during Prohibition this was not the case. But alcohol plays a strong part in many of the violent deaths — the murders and suicides, as well as the fatal accidents — that occur in slum neighborhoods. Some people deliberately get drunk to get up the courage to do something illegal or violent. Many studies have shown, in fact, that if it were not for intoxication, certain violent acts might not have occurred.

Much of the violence in the neighborhoods we have been speaking of is done by people your age. It is also far more serious than the occasional acts of vandalism, the housebreaks, and the car thefts that are common among youth in other neighborhoods. Murder and assault, either in gang warfare or against a member of a family, occur regularly. Sometimes, young people behave violently because of the violence they see around them; it is an expected and accepted response to certain situations, as normal as a verbal argument in a more subdued environment. Sometimes, youths commit violent acts to prove they are not chicken; again, a pressure put on them by certain members of the society in which they live. Or, a young person may act out of boredom brought on by the lack of employment and recreational opportunities. The rate of violence, we know, goes up markedly when young people find themselves hanging out with little to occupy their time, or when they have not learned to control aggression by redirecting their energy into study, hobbies, sports, or work. Instead, they may behave violently to relieve their frustrations, or to take out their anger.

But it is important to remember that society, especially the family part of it, can also put pressure on a young person by being too strict and demanding, by insisting on model behavior. Just as a child may react aggressively if parents encourage aggressive behavior, or are angry or hostile themselves, so, too, may a young person behave badly, sometimes aggressively, out of frustration brought on by continual pressure to be good. Psychologists point out that children who are overpolite, who always do the "right thing," can become emotional cripples and are apt to commit aggressive acts if they cannot or do not want to meet the high goals their parents set for them.

Perhaps the best example of violence erupting among youth from "model" homes comes from Japan, a country noted for its close family ties, diligence, courtesy, and stern educational and employment systems. Street crime as we know it in the United States is virtually unheard of in Japan; there is, however, considerable white-collar crime, such as embezzlement and fraud, as well as an occasional gangland murder. But in recent years, there have been growing instances of teenage violence; it is not directed against strangers or schoolmates, but against teachers, and against parents. A few examples: a fifteen-year-old junior high school pupil blasted apart his teacher's parked car with dynamite to avenge "embarrassing demands"; a pair of fourteen-year-olds armed with metal baseball bats severely beat their teacher after he told another student not to spit on the floor; a sixteen-year-old boy fatally beat his father so he could live happily with his sister and mother.

Such incidents might not raise an eyebrow if they occurred in the United States. But in a traditional country like Japan, where things like that are alien, they are a source of increasing concern. Hardly a day passes without a media report of a teacher assaulted with a bamboo sword or a steel pipe, of a mother savagely punched or kicked by a young son — a phenomenon peculiar to Japan and referred to by sociologists as the "battered mother syndrome" — or of students causing some disturbance in a classroom. The reasons behind the outbreaks of violence among Japan's youth are not clear. But there are some theories.

Perhaps one important factor is the growing Westernization of the country, a term used to mean that Japan is being strongly influenced by the United States and Europe. It does not mean that Japan will one day become like us — only that many of our ways are being adopted or adapted by the Japanese. Some child psychologists and police officials believe that the Western emphasis on individuality — as opposed to the Japanese high regard for group effort — and other Western ways are to blame for "infecting" Japanese youth. Rock music, American styles of dress, the more carefree attitude toward sex of young Americans — each of these has been blamed by the more conservative Japanese for the youth problems besetting the country. One Japanese businessman, in all seriousness, told me that he was sure U.S. youth were more aggressive because they eat so much hamburger — and he expressed grave concern that beef, which is not traditional fare in Japan, was being consumed in increasing quantities in his country, and with obvious delight, by Japanese teenagers.

But blaming outside influences for the violent behavior among Japan's youth is far too simple; it is an easy way to divert attention from the more important causes to be found within Japanese society itself. It is true that the influence of the West, which defeated Japan in World War II, has been enormous. But it has been more positive than negative, considering how the United States and its allies helped rebuild a nation they destroyed. It is also true that what has been called the "future shock" of too many changes too soon in a society not far removed from the days it was ruled by shoguns has confused young people, who are now trying to live in both a modern and an old world.

There is nearly unanimous agreement that many Japanese youths are behaving violently because they are rebelling against tradition, and against a competitive school system that is conducted, in the words of one official of the Japan Teachers' Union, in an atmosphere of commands, orders, regulations, and penalties. The rules are, indeed, strict: stiff, black, military-cut uniforms for the boys; long black skirts for the girls; no smoking, no true expression of views, no wandering from the lesson plan of the teacher. There is often physical and mental abuse of the students: in one incident, a thirty-year-old junior high school teacher was accused of punching eighteen of his first-year pupils and pouring water over their heads because they failed to report a smoking incident. Moreover, competition among junior high school students seeking to gain admittance to prestigious high schools is fierce — and there is even fiercer competition for entrance to elite universities, where generations have been molded into the celebrated Japanese workaholics who devote their lives to a single company.

But it is not only the stern teacher who goads the

pupils. At home, the mother is charged with her children's education, and for pushing her son — in Japan, a male child still receives the most favorable educational opportunities, and later more high-level professional opportunities than women — in the right direction. As well-meaning as she may be, the Japanese mother, according to some psychologists, creates problems because she not only drives her child toward achievement, but also often allows herself to be blackmailed by him, giving him what he wants in return for studying. As one junior high student complained, "How can we live like this? Why don't teachers and parents allow us to relax and appreciate human relationships and love? Because of this atmosphere at home and school — study, study, study — we feel as though our frustration and anger are about to explode." And explode they often do — against teachers and mothers. One newspaper survey found that 40 percent of junior high students wanted to strike their teachers, and 60 percent said the teachers were to blame when they were struck.

Regarding violence in the United States, police officials point out that most youths who lash out at parents are from good homes, and have fine records at school. That observation, which debunks the popular idea that bad kids come only from unstable homes, was echoed recently in a six-year U.S. government study of why American teenagers get into trouble with the law. Interestingly, the study, which was supported by the Justice Department, found that broken homes seemed to have little to do with molding a juvenile delinquent; but it did find that teenagers who hold jobs or drive cars are at high risk of running afoul of the law. "It was not an early driver's license per se that resulted in police contacts," the study said, "but simply having access to the automobile, just as early employment may have exposed some juveniles to greater risk and also given them funds to be spent in a trouble-producing way during the years of socialization."[13]

The violence that erupted on our nation's campuses during the sixties had little to do with bad homes. College students, for the most part, do not return at night to ghetto homes, nor are they usually abused and unloved by their parents. The things that caused the student riots were issues in which the participants believed strongly. When the students' aims were thwarted — whether these were to end the unpopular Vietnam War or assure equal rights for minorities — their frustrations exploded into violence.

It was mentioned earlier that families often set high goals, and that when some young people are unable or unwilling to meet those goals they become angry and aggressive. Society, too, can also set high goals that sometimes cause certain people to turn violent. A good example of that occurs when a very successful person, a person who has made the most of what society offered or asked of him, is murdered by a resentful assassin. Angry that "someone" or "something" prevented him from achieving greatness, the assassin may lash out at the person who symbolizes "making it," be he or she a rock singer or movie star, or the boss, or the fellow student who always gets A's. When Beatle John Lennon was shot to death by young Mark David Chapman, one psychologist commented, "Lennon, with his expensive apartments, and happy marriage, represented a symbol of stability and success that the killer himself wanted."[14] Thus, as a result of murdering someone like Lennon, the killer is no longer inferior but is now a celebrity himself, someone in the public eye.

But, as this chapter makes clear, society and all the other environmental pressures are not the only factors that must be considered, especially in cases like the Lennon murder, or in any of the other so-called senseless slayings that we hear and read so much about. The environment, remember, is but the match that ignites the powder in the firecracker. And in that powder, deep in our bodies, may be just the right mix of ingredients, from brain chemicals to chromosomes to individual peculiarities like low self-esteem and poor sense of identity, even envy, all of which can set some people off.

Let's begin our study of that "powder" by looking at the single bodily organ crucial to behavior, violent or peaceful, the brain. It is the center of interest for researchers who study what they refer to as the "biology of violence." This three-pound spongy mass, this organic model for the program-packed computer, bears the imprints that the environment, the things that other people say and do, leaves on all of us. The information, favorable and unfavorable, that is stamped into our brains starts seeping in when we are young; it can come from outside, or we may be born with it. If there is an overload of wrong information, of unfavorable environmental signals, chances are the young brain will not develop properly, and the child, and later the adult, may become aggressive.

To appreciate how this can happen, you should understand that the brain is more than a reasoning, living organ. It is also an intricate electrical instrument that is in charge of an elaborate network of billions of nerve cells, interconnecting nerve branches, and the spinal cord, over which electrical messages are sent out and received and that regulate our actions and behavior. The nerve cells contain electrical charges caused by chemicals. So important are these electrochemicals that without them we could not move, smell, hear, see, or feel; every time we use one of these senses, electrochemical messages are beaming back and forth from the brain to all parts of the body. Put a hand on a hot stove, goes the old example, and pain nerves are stimulated; they transmit an electrical pulse to the brain, a message that says, in effect, "It hurts." Instantly, the brain sends a message to the hand, directing it to pull away from the stove.

The brain is divided into two sections, each of which is subdivided into five other sections, or lobes. Since certain portions of the brain are responsible for specific activities — bodily movements, balance, coordination, language, memory — damage to these portions can upset the normal function that each governs. When the frontal lobe is damaged, for example, personality changes can occur; injury to another lobe, the occipital, can cause blindness. Scientists know, too, that "electrical storms" — erratic shifts in the normal, distinctive brain-wave pattern that occurs during the discharge of electrical current — take place in the center of the brain's temporal lobe, the main site of impulse control, when a person has certain disorders, such as epilepsy. These "storms" are believed to be behind the strange behavior such as outbursts of violence that some epileptics demonstrate. Some of these storms may originate deeper in the brain, in the area known as the limbus, believed to be the center of our brains early in evolution; this primitive system has long been associated with our emotions, and it controls and directs many kinds of behavior.

Some years ago, researchers at the Massachusetts General Hospital in Boston — Drs. Vernon Mark and Frank Ervin — demonstrated the role these brainstorms play in violent behavior. They first implanted electrodes in the brains of various laboratory animals, and then passed an electric current into the brains. "By varying the radio frequency," Dr. Ervin reported, "we can play right up and down the ladder of emotions in these animals, stimulating a cat, for instance, to the point where it would attack anything in front of it, be it a mouse, a ball or a tiger."[15]

Similar reactions have been produced in humans. Moreover, by applying electricity to the site of the brainstorms, it is possible to actually turn off the anger and aggressiveness in certain patients by destroying tiny bits of brain tissue at the site of the storms. (This is called bloodless surgery.) This ability to turn violent behavior on or off with electrical stimulation, along with the discovery that storms are present during outbursts by certain patients, supports the idea that electrical disorders are at the core of much of today's violence. In a book on violence and the brain, Drs. Mark and Ervin made it clear that they were concerned with *personal* violent behavior — unwarranted and usually unprovoked acts that attempt to or actually do injure or destroy another person or thing. "We are all too familiar with this sort of violence," they wrote. "It has been highlighted by political assassinations . . . it also underlies the wanton slayings and senselessly enraged reactions of bad drivers, muggers, barroom brawlers, child beaters, and rapists who supply our newspapers with sensational copy and help make our streets, homes, cars and airplanes unsafe. And although other animals also indulge in violent behavior, the repertoire of individual violence and the social environment within which it occurs are uniquely characteristic of the human species."[16]

In stressing the role of the brain in violent behavior, the two researchers do not deny the importance of social influences on behavior. They wrote:

> We are well aware of the economic and social injustices that drive groups of people to riot and rebellion; the increasing sense of alienation and frustration that pervades our technological society; and the provocative accounts and depictions of violence to which we are daily exposed in papers and magazines, or on movie and television screens. Nor are we discounting the effects of education, personal history, evolutionary heritage, genetic endowment, and individual biological and psychological makeup. The fact is, however, that all these influences and events impinge on, are stored in, and are translated

into behavior patterns solely by the brain — so that no matter from what point we start, we always come back to that organ's primary importance. It is our belief that until we understand more about how brain activity is reflected in behavior, we will not fully understand what causes individual violence.[17]

The doctors wisely point out that the theories about violence that focus on human nature and its interactions with environment — as well as our attitudes toward criminals, the law, and personal responsibility — always take for granted that every person has a healthy, normally functioning brain. "Most people consider brain disease to be a rare phenomenon," they observe. "It is likely, however, that more than 10 million Americans suffer from an obvious brain disease, and the brains of perhaps another five million have been subtly damaged. We do not mean to say that all of these brain-diseased people are violent. What we are saying is that an appreciable percentage of the relatively few individuals guilty of repeated personal violence are to be found in this five to 10 percent of the population whose brains do not function in a perfectly normal way."[18]

More recently, the part the brain plays in violent behavior was demonstrated in a study conducted by Vanderbilt University psychiatrist Dr. William Petrie. The study is interesting because, rather than dealing with violence committed by youths or hardened criminals, it focused on violence done by the elderly, a group almost always regarded as the victim of violence. Dr. Petrie found that 139 patients surveyed in a state psychiatric hospital had committed or threatened violence, with or without weapons. Eighteen of the patients, he reported in the *Journal of the American Medical Association,* had committed violent acts, twelve with guns; these patients, who had a mean age of nearly 74 years, were classified for the purpose of the study as violent; 121 had committed or threatened violence without using weapons, and were categorized as aggressive rather than violent.[19]

According to Dr. Petrie, the aggressive patients were more likely to have behavior problems caused by brain-tissue damage. Many had degenerative brain disease accompanied by memory loss, time and place disorientation, and general confusion. Their outbursts were reflexive — rather than premeditated — and were less likely to be dangerous. Most of the violent patients, on the other hand, had paranoid delusions — a mental illness characterized by fear and suspicion — unaccompanied by demonstrated brain-tissue damage; unlike the aggressive patients, they were not confused or disoriented and were capable of premeditated acts.

Antipsychotic drugs that interact with brain chemicals to alter mood are often used to treat violent behavior, and this may be taken as further proof of the brain's important role in violence. Such drugs are given to treat disorders like schizophrenia, one of the human race's greatest mental cripplers. The disorder can be controlled to some extent, but if it is untreated it can cause the sufferer to do violence both to himself or herself, and to others. While the environment has been blamed for years, many researchers now believe than an error in the body's chemistry, probably inherited and that produces poisonous substances that affect the brain just as overdoses of drugs and alcohol do, is at fault. Some of these poisons have been found in the blood and urine of schizophrenics, and when they are injected into laboratory animals they cause many of the behavioral changes characteristic of the disease of schizophrenia. Other chemicals have been injected experimentally into the brains of rats, cats, and monkeys to produce killer impulses and fits of rage, and to suppress them. In one experiment conducted a few years ago at Princeton University, rats that normally never killed mice did so after they were injected with a drug that mimics a naturally occurring brain chemical believed to help transmit nerve impulses. What was even more astonishing was that when the rats killed, they did so in exactly the same way that other naturally aggressive rats might kill — with a bite in the back of the neck — even though they had never seen other rats kill.

Another important consideration about the biology of violence is the role of the chromosomes, those thin strands of the genetic material called DNA (deoxyribonucleic acid). Their number varies in each plant and animal cell nucleus: two, for instance, in a lowly worm, four in a garden pea, forty-six in human beings. Our sex is determined by two chromosomes, designated X and Y, because they actually look like those letters when viewed under a microscope. Ordinarily, the female has sex chromosomes designated XX, and the normal male, XY. But sometimes, the male makeup goes wrong, becoming XXY instead of XY, with the error weighted toward femaleness. There is also an error in the opposite direction — XYY. The extra Y chromosome results in what is sometimes referred to as supermaleness. Men with this extra Y chromosome are unusually tall, somewhat retarded, highly sexually motivated, and they may be more aggressive than normal males. The error occurs once in every 2,000 male births.

Much attention has been focused on the man with the extra Y chromosome, and researchers have been trying for a long time to find out more about the Y error's connection to violent behavior. In 1965, studies done on nearly two hundred violently criminal Scots turned up seven XYY cases in the group. There was also the case of a French stable hand who murdered a prostitute, and was later found to have XYY chromosomes. And there was speculation that a man named Richard Speck, convicted of killing eight Chicago nurses some years ago, had the XYY makeup.

Because of such cases, many scientists have concluded — though not without some reservation — that criminals, especially the criminally insane, have more mistakes in their sex chromosomes than can be accounted for by chance alone. The extra Y chromosome, of course, raises a number of questions. If a syndrome is established, is the criminal who has it less morally or legally responsible for his crimes? Can the syndrome be used as a defense in a murder trial? One must wonder, too, what would become of, say, infants who during medical screening for some genetic disorder were found to have this "criminal chromosome." Critics of the emphasis that has been placed on the extra Y chromosome argue that such infants would be discriminated against the rest of their lives, and so, too, would their families. It is not difficult to understand, given the climate of suspicion and fear in a violent age, how the neighbors and even the families of the extra Y chromosome child might feel about the chromosomal abnormality. Critics also maintain that since nothing can be done about the extra Y chromosome anyway — short of banishing anyone who has one — merely identifying it would do no good.

The controversy over the extra Y chromosome crops up every so often. Some researchers recently claimed that it may not necessarily make a man directly violent; rather, they say, XYY men may have learning disabilities and lower intelligence, and that these disadvantages may be what starts them on a life of crime. Others believe that the XYY male who is violent probably got that way only if he inherited the extra chromosome from an aggressive father — in other words, if the father was a peaceful man, the extra Y would not make much difference. In any event, not enough research has been done to definitely blame a message in the genes for violent behavior.

Other studies in the biology of violence concentrate on the role of hormones, chemicals that originate in the endocrine glands and circulate in the bloodstream to various parts of the body, regulating certain physical reactions, and affecting our emotions. They are a potent force indeed. When, for example, the hormone adrenaline pours through the blood in times of stress, it drives up blood pressure, makes the heart beat faster and the muscles tense; it is called the "fight or flight" hormone because it works during emergency situations. Testosterone, the male hormone produced by the male sex glands, is responsible for such male characteristics as deep voice, hair growth, and the function of certain reproductive organs; estrogen, the female sex hormone, governs the development of breasts and the onset of menstruation, to name two functions.

It is known that hormonal changes can stimulate or hold back aggressive behavior in humans. A few years ago, a study conducted at Rutgers University found that giving synthetic sex hormones, especially those responsible for development of masculine characteristics, to prevent miscarriage may increase the potential for aggressive behavior in male and female offspring.[20] In the study, the effects on real life behavior appeared to be positive — that is, the children seemed to do better in school and in athletics. On the other hand, synthetic sex hormones can have a negative effect. Another study found that boys whose mothers had been treated with a sex hormone were subject to more disciplinary action in school than boys whose mothers had not had the hormone treatment; the daughters of hormone-treated mothers grew more angry more often, and with more intensity than other girls. From such studies, many scientists conclude that some of the very aggressive people in our society may be that way because of a combination of various environmental factors and excessive hormones that begin to build up prior to birth.

The relationship between sex and aggression is an interesting one. Scientists who study animal behavior know, for instance, that fighting among some male animals occurs mostly during the periods when their sex hormones are being released, a time when many of them develop bright colors that attract females and competitors alike. Monkey studies also show that the male monkeys who dominate — that is, the ones who take the lead and are the most aggressive — have higher testosterone levels than the more passive ones. Moreover, when one of these dominant male monkeys is beaten in a fight by one of the lesser monkeys, the winner will now have a higher testosterone level than the monkey he has defeated.

In human beings, a male's sexual desires, the result of what has been described as a "hormonal flood," can be channeled into sports, hobbies, or schoolwork — or, they can, if frustrated, show themselves in violent contact sports and fighting. Some studies have also suggested that exposing a male to pornography can cause him to be aggressive. While there is a difference of opinion over whether or not pornography is linked to the commission of sex crimes, some investigators have found that highly aggressive erotic material may make a man more aggressive toward a woman, especially if he is inclined toward such behavior. Others doubt, however, that pornography is an important consideration in cases like rape. Most rapists, as shall be seen in a later discussion of rape, are motivated by other emotions, including rage and the need to feel powerful. Nonetheless, it is difficult to discount the effect certain vivid portrayals have on us all, especially when we are growing up.

This, of course, leads us to one of the most controversial topics in any discussion of violent behavior — the role of television, movies, and other forms of entertainment in fanning aggression.

Let's begin by stating firmly that not all the violent entertainment to which we are exposed will damage our minds and turn us into strong-armed savages. *Hamlet* and *Macbeth* are, after all, quite violent, and these are not banned. Reading accounts of the violent acts committed by the English kings, Roman emperors, and the Christian crusaders do not influence us adversely — in fact, the exploits of these people of the past may even make some of us proud. And who would dare to say seriously that the child's tale "Jack and the Beanstalk" should be censored? — even though Jack is a rather nasty lad who trespasses on a giant's property, robs him of a hen that lays golden eggs, a talking harp, and bags of diamonds, then kills him, for trying only to regain what was taken illegally from him. No, far from harming us emotionally, the fictional violence of literature and the very real violence of history entertain, thrill, and teach us. One reason that such accounts do not bother us is that we are far removed from them.

As mentioned previously, children who have been abused often become abusers themselves when they grow up. They have had firsthand experience with violence. On the other hand, the aggressive acts we read about or watch on television and in the movies are only reflections of events that are true or imagined. They are unreal and distant shadows. Another reason we are usually untouched by such portrayals is that most of us do not have a steady diet of them. Just about anything, from salt to sex, from play to work, can injure us physically or mentally if we have too much of it. Fortunately, most of us vary our activities and our diets, as well as our reading and other forms of entertainment. Finally, unless what we read or see actually glorifies the violence, makes it something to be admired and imitated, it is doubtful that it will have an evil effect on most of us. If, for example, young people are continually exposed to stories that portray drug dealing, murder, robbery, and adultery as acceptable, then chances are that their moral values will be twisted somewhat; if the writer or the family or friends intervene by raising arguments, when appropriate, against unlawful, socially unacceptable behavior, then the chances are that any adverse effect of certain story material will be lessened if not eliminated altogether.

So the question of whether written or filmed accounts of violence — especially on television because it is so accessible — affect our behavior cannot really be answered with a simple yes or no. The nature and intensity of the violence depicted, the frequency of exposure, and the age of the person exposed to it are all very important considerations. So much has been written about television's impact on youth that it is difficult to sift the reason from the hysteria. Sociologists and psychiatrists, television network executives, religious leaders, and parents' organizations have all had something to say on the subject. For some, television, at its worst, is an assault on a child's mind, an insidious influence that upsets moral balance and makes a child prone to aggressive behavior as it warps his or her perception of the real world. Others see television as an unhealthy intrusion into a child's learning process, substituting easy pictures for the discipline of reading and concentrating, and transforming the young viewer into a hypnotized nonthinker. On still another side are those who feel that television's impact has been grossly overestimated; they feel it has enormous potential for educating, especially those who cannot abide the traditional forms of learning; and they argue that when properly controlled, television programming and viewing hours are beneficial, not only for learning about the world and human relations, but for pure entertainment and relaxation. As far as its aggression-provoking potential is concerned, those in the pro-TV camp often argue that fictional violence actually helps children face violence in a healthy way without denial and overprotection, and may even dissipate aggression.

As noted earlier, aggression is largely learned behavior. If you accept that argument, then it is hard to deny that television is a way to learn aggression. But it all depends on who is watching what and how often. Professional soldiers and policemen, for example, who are trained to act violently on occasion do not go about beating people up as a matter of course. Nor do average adults who occasionally watch and enjoy violence on TV, appreciating it for the unreality it is, run out and murder or assault someone. But, when we talk about young people, it is a very different matter.

It should be fairly obvious that a young, impressionable child who watches several hours of unsupervised television every day will probably be affected adversely, given the high frequency of violence, both in the weekend cartoon programs and in the programs for adults. Estimates of the amount of television violence carried by the networks vary, but there is enough of it to make one wonder if TV is interested in anything else. For instance, Dr. Randall P. Harrison, a professor of communication at Michigan State University and a psychologist at the University of California, noted that the average American child in the ten-year period between the ages of five and fifteen sees some 13,400 human beings destroyed on the TV screen. "In growing up," he wrote in a publication of the American Academy of Pediatrics, "the typical child spends as much time with television as he does in our educational system. He spends more of his waking hours watching TV than in any other single activity."[21] Other surveys indicate that adults in the United States watch roughly thirty-three hours of television a week, children about thirty. In 1982, U.S. Surgeon General C. Everett Koop reported that exposure to violent scenes on television and in the movies was a key factor in stimulating youth violence. Referring to a 1981 report by the California Commission on Crime Control and Violence Prevention, he noted that the study estimated that by the time young people reached eighteen, they could have witnessed some eighteen thousand murders.[22] And in 1983, a primetime study by the Media Institute, a research group in Washington, found an average of 1.7 overwhelmingly violent crimes per show programmed on ABC, CBS, and NBC. The researchers also found that murders were more than a hundred times as frequent on TV as in real life. But, the report noted, in this fantasy world most criminals were thwarted and crime was punished — something that does not always happen in real life. That may or may not be a plus, though as has been indicated, if crime is portrayed in an unfavorable light or when arguments are presented against it, chances are a young person will not be harmed by it. It may not be a plus, however, because, as it has been argued, even if a criminal is made to pay, even though one of the "good guys" punishes the wrongdoer, when violence is used to solve a problem it still makes violence acceptable behavior; in other words, if wrongdoing is dealt with violently, then it is an easy jump to justify one's own violent behavior in certain situations.

Several studies and reports have shown that television violence can lead to aggressive behavior in children and adolescents. A surgeon general's report found some "preliminary indications of a causal relationship between television viewing and aggressive behavior in children." Ten years later, the National Institute of Mental Health found a similar connection, adding that primetime TV carried an average of five violent acts an hour, compared to eighteen per hour on children's weekend programming. In Dr. Harrison's aforementioned report, he cited a research project in which children were left to monitor the videotaped play of other children, and were told to call the experimenter if things got out of hand. "In the video sequence, which the child thought was actual children in another room at the same time," said Dr. Harrison, "things did, indeed, get out of hand. Progressively more mayhem began to take place.

Those children who had just seen commercial television violence accepted much higher levels of aggression than those who had not."[23]

In another study referred to by Dr. Harrison, researchers went back and studied the same children who ten years before had participated in a research project involving televised violence. "In their followup research, these investigators found some startling relationships between TV violence in the third grade and aggressive behavior ten years later," said Dr. Harrison. "The research design is complex, but it appears that there is a causal link between the amount of TV violence a child sees at eight or nine, and the aggressiveness he exhibits at eighteen or nineteen. In short, if your eight-year-old watches a lot of TV violence, you can predict — better than chance — that you'll shape him into an aggressive child."[24]

In still another study, researchers observed a significant rise in the level of physical and verbal aggression among children in a community when television was introduced for the first time. In yet another, a British researcher found that long exposure to televised violence may slowly and unconsciously undermine the inhibitions learned from society. The investigator, Dr. William A. Belson, evaluated some fifteen hundred boys aged thirteen to sixteen and determined that the ones who had heavy TV exposure were nearly 50 percent more likely to commit serious violent acts than boys whose exposure was light. The heavy TV viewers were also more likely to commit violent acts in general. Said a report of the study, "Certain types of programs were more likely to lead to serious violent behavior than others; among the worst offenders were programs which featured physical or verbal violence in close personal relationships, programs with gratuitous violence not arising out of the plot, realistic fictional violence, violence done by the 'good guys' and violent Westerns."[25]

However, watching violent sports (except boxing or wrestling), science fiction, cartoons, or slapstick comedies did not increase serious violence. Moreover, the report concluded, a survey of attitudes showed that TV violence did not increase callousness, acceptance of violence as a solution to problems, or the feeling that violence is inevitable. "This finding suggests," said the report, "that the effects of TV violence are more subtle than a simple change in attitude."[26]

The effects of filmed violence, however, can sometimes be deadly. A few years ago, the movie *The Deer Hunter*, a violent film in which the Vietnam War figures prominently, created a stir. Especially troubling was a scene in which American prisoners are forced to play Russian roulette, a game of chance in which all the chambers of a pistol are empty except one; the "player" puts the gun to his head and, not knowing which chamber contains the bullet, pulls the trigger. After the film was shown on television, some fifteen Russian roulette deaths were reported throughout the United States, apparently of people who had imitated the movie scene. In an article on the phenomenon, the *Christian Science Monitor* ran the headline: "Is This Movie Killing People?" The paper pointed out that though the film had been shown in movie houses across the country, no killings traceable to its showing in the theaters had been reported. The question arose as to whether the home environment and the accessibility of handguns combined to create a situation unique to television watching. A reporter asked Dr. Thomas Radecki, an Illinois psychiatrist who headed the National Coalition on TV Violence, for comment. Said Dr. Radecki, "I can speculate there might be something in the home environment. . . . For someone seeing it in a more alien or foreign location, a movie theater, it may not be psychologically experienced as part of their real life. (One victim killed at twenty-four) happened to have a revolver sitting next to him — very few people take a revolver into a theater. For most people (seeing it in a theater) there is a time lapse of several hours to several days (before they have access to a gun)."[27]

The newspaper also quoted Linda Talbott of Handgun Control as saying, "This film was shown all over the country in theaters and we didn't see any imitations. Suddenly it's shown on TV and there's imitation. Marshall McLuhan (the Canadian educator) has pointed out the mesmerizing hypnotic effect of the (TV) medium. The data coming in suggests that (when watching a film on TV) the normal judgment mechanisms are not operating the same way. The accessibility factor (presence of a gun) is great. People who go to theaters are generally aware that their concept of reality is being suspended. But TV is right there in your own home; it's as though the line between reality and fantasy is blurred."[28]

This does not mean that violent films seen in theaters

and drive-ins are always harmless. Everyone has seen, or certainly knows of, the more bloody ones that make full use of new special effects to realistically dismember victims; the tools of such slaughter range from chainsaws to airplane propellers. Strangely, such films are rarely X-rated, though censors are quick to pin such a label on films that are deemed too sexually explicit. For one reason or another, sexual acts are often regarded as more apt to injure a youngster's mind and alter his or her behavior than those that are repulsively and obscenely violent. The respected film critic Janet Maslin has had this to say about the filmed bloodbaths that debase both the movies and their audiences: "Go see one, and you'll have empirical proof that a film like this makes audiences mean. You will leave the theater convinced that the world is an ugly, violent place in which aggression is frequent and routine. Lurid headlines in the tabloids will seem positively realistic; after watching a dozen young vacationers being garrotted, the news of, say, a gunman on the loose in a hospital ward will sound comparatively harmless. Violence in the real world becomes much more acceptable after you've seen infinitely greater violence on the screen. . . . This latest kind of pornography — violent pornography — doesn't even begin to allow its audience the catharsis of the traditional horror story. Such catharsis isn't what these films are after, and truly cathartic horror needn't be as explicit or literal as this. And in fact, the extreme gore works against any possibility of release, since it deadens the audience and creates a feeling of utter hopelessness. These films aim simply at shocking and numbing their audiences, and perhaps the only good thing to be said about them is that their future isn't bright. Like sexual pornography, violent pornography has its implicit limitations, and it's gone about as far as it can go."[29]

What is to be done about the hideous brutality that so often appears on TV and on movie film? Some have suggested stronger censorship laws, a move that could not only violate freedom of press and speech rights but might make the banned films more appealing; it might also drive promoters and producers underground, where they would continue to churn them out for customers unwilling to be deprived of their right to see what they want. True, children might be prevented from watching such films by simply banning them; but in a democratic society, such heavy-handed tactics could have serious repercussions. Other suggestions include better program scheduling to keep particularly violent movies and teleplays off television during hours when children would be most apt to watch. Parental discretion, of course, is an important factor — that is, a parent makes the decision about what or whether a child should watch. But, this doesn't always mean that if a mother or father says it's okay that it is. Parents can be wrong, too. Nor does watching television as a family always lessen the impact of the violence. In one study of elementary schoolchildren a few years ago, it was shown that the level of aggression touched off by a violent TV program was the same when an adult was present or absent, and whether the adult expressed approval or disapproval of the violence. Nonetheless, the study did indicate that the way in which a child's aggression was expressed — that is, whether he or she let it out, held it in, or avoided it — was influenced by the adult. In the study, children who were in a group in which the adult approved of the violence on TV, and children in a group in which the adult expressed disapproval, were given tests after the shows to measure how they handled aggression. The children whose adult partners approved of the violence demonstrated aggression more openly than the others. Although the children whose adult partners disapproved of the TV violence did not display aggression as openly, they had more internalized, or withheld, aggression than the others.[30]

Nonetheless, others who have thought about how best to cope with television programming that may be injurious to a young person's mental health conclude that critical judgment from parents is imperative. Moreover, expressions of concern from parents are more important than how much television is watched or what restrictions are placed on what children watch. A few years ago, media specialists at the University of Texas at Austin examined how families could deal with TV. In emphasizing critical judgment by parents, English professor Horace M. Newcomb pointed out that such judgments could be as mild as a parent's saying, "Ah, that's unrealistic," to comments like, "You know that is not the way families deal with questions," or, "You recognize that police don't actually work that way." Such an approach, according to Newcomb, gives a child an opening either to ask a question or simply to take the idea into his or her own head and begin to work on it. Said he, "It's the totally uncritical acceptance of TV that is worrisome."[31]

Television, of course, is not the most important reason people turn violent. But it is a factor, and researchers understand this well enough to continue looking into its effects. Television also has great potential as a teaching tool. As one woman put it in a letter to the Los Angeles *Herald Examiner,* "Television is the greatest and most powerful medium the world has ever seen — for never before has it been possible to communicate and influence millions and millions of people at the same moment right in their own homes. But its misuse has been criminal, for which society is now paying an increasing price."[32]

·2·

GROUP VIOLENCE

*There is no grievance that is a fit object of
redress by mob law.*

— ABRAHAM LINCOLN

VIOLENCE CAN BE DONE by individuals with their own private motives, and by individuals working for the motives of a special group. Many times, when one person assaults another it is for highly personal reasons: a drug dealer murders an undercover agent to escape arrest, a woman kills a lover who has been cheating on her to punish him and the other woman, an irate employee murders the manager who fired him, a young man provokes a brawl to prove he is tough, a woman is raped because her attacker was once spurned by a high school girlfriend and now hates all women.

But quite often, individuals commit violent acts not only to satisfy themselves but also to gain some benefit for a group of people. They may belong to a lynch mob that takes the law into its own hands and executes a suspect before he or she has had a fair trial; they may be members of a secret society of misguided zealots that uses violence to intimidate; they may be participants in a family feud, a private war waged for generations to avenge the death of one of its members long ago; they may be political terrorists who use violence to force change, or to call attention to their cause, or to avenge some real or imagined or long-past insult or wrong. Some people may not even be members of the group for whom they commit violence: a hired assassin, for instance, might not be at all concerned with the philosophy or actions of the world leader he has been paid to eliminate, nor have any personal grudge against him. But whether such hired killers formally belong to an organization is not all that important; their reasons for maiming and killing are usually to further the aims of that group.

Let us begin our discussion of group violence by looking at what psychologists call crowd behavior, popularly known as mob psychology. Certainly, there are no formal membership requirements, no dues to be paid, to join a lynch mob or a student riot. Unlike some of the other forms of group violence to be discussed later, mob violence is often unplanned and unorganized; a mob's members lose their ability to think rationally, so intent are they on acting as one; its leadership generally depends on who can shout the loudest, or who is strong enough to get to the front of the crowd fastest. Moreover, a mob generally breaks up rather quickly once its purpose has been achieved. Says one sociology textbook, "In crowd behavior, irrational as it always is, the impulse to follow a suggested course of action is obeyed at once; whereas, in any form of rational behavior, there is always delay enough to permit comparisons and evaluations."[1]

Experts in mob psychology say the anatomy of a riot

begins with a precipitating event, a trigger. This may be the arrest of someone the crowd believes to be innocent or a scapegoat; an assault on a white by a black, or vice versa; a simple official act, like the dedication of a statue of a controversial figure; the parking of a foreign car near an automobile factory that suffered high unemployment because of foreign-car imports; or merely the announcement that a state has approved the construction of a nuclear power plant.

As word of the triggering event spreads, the crowd becomes angrier; finally, violence erupts, escalating from shouting and occasional rock throwing to open street war as the rioters clash with police, others in authority, or those who oppose their views. Such a situation has been compared to the outbreak of a disease epidemic. Dr. John P. Spiegel, who headed the Lemberg Center for the Study of Violence at Brandeis University, once said of mass violence, "You just can't ignore it, isolate it, or hope that it will cure itself."[2]

Often, the common hostility of a crowd has been festering for some time, and is not just a sudden eruption. If, for instance, a hostile mob has gathered at a civil rights parade, the concerted action taken when some incident or person ignites the violence is the result of a long-standing racial conflict simmering in each member of the crowd. Matters are obviously made much worse, and the mob becomes more inflamed, if whatever it is that provokes the riot has not been dealt with fairly, or at all, by authorities.

A mob generally behaves in ways that its individual members would shun if alone: few members of a riotous crowd would, for example, stand alone in front of a policeman and shout obscenities at him; nor would many people break a store window in broad daylight and help themselves to a television set or a wristwatch; and it is highly unlikely that mob members would, acting alone, attempt to crash a gate at a navy base to protest the docking of a nuclear submarine. It is the *gathering* of individuals, with their strong, shared feeling, that gives the individuals within the group their sense of courage and power, and allows each to release impulses usually kept under control. Wartime and periods of insurrection contain proof of that. For example, on Easter Monday in 1282, on the island of Sicily, a riot broke out after a French soldier insulted a Sicilian woman in front of a church at the hour of evening worship, or vespers; in what came to be known as the Sicilian Vespers, the riot swelled to a political revolt against the Angevin French who ruled the island, and virtually the entire French population was murdered. In Nanking, China, during World War II, drunken Japanese soldiers and sailors slaughtered 150,000 Chinese and raped some 5,000 women in an outbreak of mob brutality that seems almost inconceivable.

Mob action, like the violence it spawns, is not new. Dissent has a long history, and mobs have gathered since at least the early Roman days — when loud protests were lodged even then against the high cost of living — to air economic, political, and social grievances, or to vent their anger against other groups. In China in 1900, for example, a branch of a sect known as the White Lotus — also called Boxers — rose up against foreigners. Missionaries were murdered, a German official was assassinated, and later some two hundred foreigners were driven to seek refuge in the British legation. They were besieged by the Boxers for two months, and were finally rescued by an expedition of soldiers from America, Great Britain, France, Germany, Russia, and Japan. A few years later, on January 22, 1905, Russian peasant workers marched on Saint Petersburg to present a petition to the czar. They were attacked by the czar's troops and hundreds of unarmed workers were killed.

In the United States, mobs turned against immigrants, especially Orientals and Irish Catholics, in the 1800s. Native-born Americans, fearful that the immigrants would gain political power, and angry that they were taking jobs for cheaper pay, regularly attacked the immigrants in the streets. During the same period, bloody labor riots erupted in cities across the United States, and many lives were lost. In 1886, for instance, there was the celebrated Haymarket riot in Chicago. It occurred when police tried to break up a labor protest meeting organized by anarchists — people who believe that all forms of government are unnecessary and undesirable. Someone threw a bomb, killing seven policemen and wounding seventy other people. A few years later, during the so-called Homestead strike at the Carnegie Steel Company plant in Pennsylvania, an armed clash took place between workers and detectives hired by the company; a number of men were killed, and soon after, the state militia had to be sent in to restore order.

Even today, workers are sometimes set upon. In

1983, when a group of independent truckers went on strike, thousands of trucks that defied the strike and kept on rolling were damaged by rocks thrown from bridges, by nails spread on the highways, and by gunfire. Many drivers were injured and one was killed.

Race has also been a factor in mob violence. During World War I (1914–1918), many blacks took jobs in defense factories. The whites were afraid that the blacks would take their jobs and move into white neighborhoods. Several violent incidents occurred — the worst in East Saint Louis in 1917 when some forty blacks and ten whites were killed during a riot. Similar racial violence broke out after World War II (1939–1945) and has continued through the years. Among the worst in recent years were the riots in the Watts section of Los Angeles in 1965, and in Newark and Detroit in 1967.

In the sixties and seventies, mob violence was common during the student protests against the war in Vietnam (1957–1975). In one of the largest such demonstrations, thousands of young people gathered in Chicago during the 1968 Democratic National Convention and battled with police in the streets. Around the same time, militant black students regularly resorted to violence to back up demands for more Afro-American history and culture courses in their colleges.

But of all this mob violence, the two incidents that stand out in recent years, perhaps for the emotional impact they had on Americans, were the tragic student deaths at Kent State University in Ohio in 1970, and the riot at Attica state prison in New York the following year. The two events were unrelated — the Kent State incident came during demonstrations against President Nixon's decision to send U.S. forces into Cambodia, and the Attica uprising stemmed from charges that inmates, most of them black, had been mistreated by white guards. But both places have become unofficial national monuments to the tragic consequences of confrontation.

The Kent State incident began with students throwing rocks, bricks, and bottles at National Guardsmen, and guardsmen firing tear gas. Then, some of the guardsmen knelt and pointed rifles at demonstrators, who shouted, "Shoot, shoot, shoot!" The kneeling guardsmen did not fire. But moments later, it happened. "I heard the first shot," one account quoted a guardsman as saying. "I had my rifle at my shoulder, not sighting, just at my shoulder. I had my finger on the trigger and fired when the others did. I just didn't think about it. It just happened. How can you think at a time like that? Right after the first shot, it sounded like everyone squeezed off one round, like at the range, drawn out. I fired once. I just closed my eyes and shot. I didn't aim at anyone in particular. I just shot at shoulder level toward the crowd." An estimated sixty shots were fired, and thirteen seconds later, when it was over, four of the student demonstrators had been killed, nine wounded. Two reporters who were there that day wrote, "Most of the victims were dressed in bell-bottoms and flowered Apache shirts, and most had Rolling Stone haircuts. Some carried books. The guardsmen wore battle helmets, gas masks, fatigues, and combat boots. The two sides looked, to each other, like the inhabitants of different worlds. . . . Blood shimmered on the grass. Bullet holes marked the trees. A generation of college students said they had lost all hope for the System and the future."[3]

The Attica incident was just as chaotic. The revolt involved some one thousand prisoners, who held thirty-eight guards and civilian workers hostage for four days. Faced with the possibility that the convicts would carry out threats to kill the hostages, New York Governor Nelson Rockefeller ordered state troopers to storm the facility. In the assault, which included use of a tear-gas-spraying helicopter, thirty-two prisoners and nine guards and employees were killed. Rockefeller, who had turned down a request that he personally visit the prison during the revolt, defended the action, saying, "There was no alternative but to go in." Adding to the depth of the tragedy were reports that many of the hostages had died of bullet wounds, rather than by knife attacks from convicts — an indication that, as commonly happens in scenes of mob violence, some people were killed unintentionally. Shortly after the riot was quelled, Rockefeller acknowledged that it was possible state troopers had killed some of the hostages. "If you recreate the circumstances of that situation — where the troopers had instructions to shoot the executioners who had been assigned to each of the prisoners [a reference to convicts menacing hostages] and who were standing there with a knife at his throat — then you add to that the helicopter coming in with the gas, and the effect of the gas — which first creates a cloud and then has an effect on the individual — you have a scene of chaos that is one in which accidents can very well happen."[4]

Both the Kent State tragedy and the awful ending to the Attica revolt raise questions about how much force should be used to put down a disturbance. Often, as has been seen, the mob itself loots and burns and kills; other times, however, it is the authorities who lose control and riot. The Boston Massacre of March 5, 1770, is a familiar example of such a situation, and one that is sometimes used when the events at Kent State are being discussed. The stationing of British soldiers in Boston in 1768 had provoked a good deal of anger among the citizens. Matters came to a head when more troops were sent to the city to protect customs commissioners. A mob of men and boys, led by a black named Crispus Attucks, began throwing missiles at the soldiers, who responded by firing into the crowd, killing five. Some witnesses regarded the unfortunate incident as a lawless affair that discredited both soldiers and the crowd; others have seen it as a historically significant event, an important preliminary to the American Revolution. Whatever it was, it lends substance to the old expression that a policeman's lot is not a happy one. "Police often vacillate between brutal suppression and inaction," said Dr. Spiegel. "If they use excessive force, they encourage the use of counterforce. If they do nothing, they encourage rioters and looters."[5]

The Kent State and Attica incidents may also make it somewhat easier to justify the violent explosion of a mob. Many people become angered after being maltreated, as at Attica, or provoked, as were the guardsmen at Kent State, and it is quite natural, although perhaps wrong, to lash out occasionally at the people believed responsible. When nobody listens to a complaint that appears to be legitimate, when nobody tries to rectify a bad situation, a violent act is perhaps the only way left to focus attention on the wrong, and help get something done about it.

When urban riots swept predominantly black cities in the North during the 1960s, many psychiatrists and psychologists suggested that blacks were releasing pent-up hostility that could not be released had they been living in the South. "The whole racial etiquette of the South was to keep the Negro male symbolically castrated for centuries," declared Dr. Alvin Poussaint, associate professor of psychiatry at Harvard University. "For any aggression the Southern Negro ever showed, the retaliatory punishment was far out of proportion to the act."[6]

But while mob action is understandable at times, there are times when it is unquestionably wrong. A lynching is an example of that. This deliberate killing, usually by hanging, of a victim who has not had a chance to defend himself, was a common occurrence in the United States from the 1800s into the late 1960s, and is a disgraceful chapter in our country's history. No one is certain about the origin of the word *lynch.* It has been attributed to James Fitz-Stevens Lynch, mayor of Galway, Ireland, who in 1493 executed his own son for murder; to an English sailor named Lynch who executed pirates without trial; to Charles Lynch, a Virginia planter who, with his neighbors in the 1700s and in defiance of the law, ordered Tories, British sympathizers, flogged; and to Lynche's Creek, a meeting place in

South Carolina for the so-called Regulators, a self-appointed group of citizens sworn to mete out justice as they saw fit.

But whatever the origin of the word, lynching has become synonymous with lawlessness and, since the vast majority of its victims were black, with bigotry gone mad. From 1889 through 1930, more than thirty-seven hundred people were lynched in the United States — over 80 percent of them blacks. (Prior to that, most lynching victims had been white. Mobs on the western frontier, without benefit of established law in those early days, resorted to lynching to punish horse thieves, highway robbers, and murderers.)

By 1968, nearly five thousand lynchings had been recorded, and, as mentioned, most of the victims were black. Lynching rates were higher in the South, and, it should go without saying, most of the lynchers were white. A look at the twenty-one lynchings that occurred in the United States in 1930 is testimony enough about the abhorrent nature of this crime. According to Richard F. Raper, who was research secretary of the Southern Commission on the Study of Lynching, the age of the victims ranged from the late teens to seventy; two-thirds of the victims were under twenty-five, ten were married. Sixteen of those killed had never before been to court; of five with criminal records, two had been charged with rape, two with theft, and one with concealing stolen goods by painting a black mule white. The alleged crimes of the victims — only one of whom had been educated beyond the fifth grade, and none of whom had been to high school — included murder, rape, robbery, attempted rape, and bombing a house.

But there was grave doubt about the guilt of eleven of the men, and two others were not even accused of any crime whatsoever. "By their very nature," Raper observed, "lynchings made it practically impossible to get at the exact facts of the alleged crimes. In practically every community with a lynching, a tradition of the absolute guilt of the person lynched sprang up immediately and cut off all further legal investigation."[7]

Many of those lynched were captured after extended manhunts organized by undeputized, armed men who used bloodhounds, and who conducted a mock trial before carrying out the executions. The victims were usually tortured, mutilated, dragged, or burned by their killers, who were mostly young men between the late teens and twenty-five. A graphic account by Raper of one vigilante killing in Georgia demonstrates the sadistic tendencies of lynchers:

"He was jabbed in his mouth with a sharp pole. His toes were cut off joint by joint. His fingers were similarly removed, and his teeth were extracted with wire pliers. After further unmentionable mutilation, the Negro's still living body was saturated with gasoline and a lighted match was applied. As the flames leaped up, hundreds of shots were fired into the dying victim. During the day, thousands of people from miles around rode out to see the sight. Not till nightfall did the officers remove the body and bury it." In another chilling example of mob frenzy, a crowd set fire to the courthouse in which the accused was held.

Members of the mob cut the water hose and thwarted the fire department's attempts to save the building. With evening, a small group of militiamen was driven from the courthouse grounds to the county jail. A little later, a larger unit of militiamen, just arrived from Dallas, was forced to retire to the protection of the jail. Shortly before midnight, with an acetylene torch and high explosives, a second-story window was blown open and the Negro's body was thrown to the crowd below. It was greeted by loud applause from the thousands who jammed the courthouse square. Police directed traffic while the corpse was dragged through the streets to a cottonwood tree in the Negro business section. There it was burned. Soon, Negro business properties valued at between $50,000 and $100,000 were fired, and the fire department was not allowed to throw water on them, though the mob permitted a hose to be trained on a white man's dwelling within fifteen feet of a burning Negro residence.[8]

Few lynchers have been brought to justice because it is quite often difficult to find the leader of such a mob. But it is also true that police officials in many of the lynching communities were indifferent to the killings; moreover, sympathetic witnesses were usually too frightened to point a finger at people responsible. But, in the last analysis, it was not only the officials and the intimidated witnesses who had to bear the burden of guilt with the actual killers — thousands of curious onlookers flocked to the lynchings, a silent mob made up of "decent folk" who, as Raper has pointed out, "provided the active mobbers with a semblance of decency and no small measure of immunity from official interference."[9]

Interestingly, New England was the only area in the

United States without a reported lynching — an admirable record until one recalls that in 1692, in Salem, Massachusetts, a hysterical persecution of "witches" and "wizards" got under way. Begun by several young girls who accused some elderly women of bewitching them, the witch-hunt resulted in many suspects being brought before a special court, and ended with nineteen of them hanged. Granted, the ignorance and prejudices of the time were to blame for such a miscarriage of justice. But it is hard to ignore the fact that group frenzy — infecting both the young women who started the inquest, and members of the court — played a part in the tragedy just as it did in the lynchings that were to take place elsewhere in the country years later.

Thus far, we have been considering unorganized, or loosely organized, group violence. But a more structured, formal sort of group violence — or more accurately, groups that approve of violence to underline their aims — has existed for centuries. Included among such organizations are those of religious fanatics, secret societies, political terrorists, and underworld "families." Each may use violent methods to instill fear, to punish, to overthrow governments or force them to change their way of thinking. Some governments, too, or conquering forces resort to violence to maintain or increase their authority and to frighten off any opposition. Such was the case during the Reign of Terror (1793–1794) in the French Revolution when nearly three thousand people of all ages were sent to the guillotine by a Committee of Public Safety dedicated to weeding out all those opposed to the Revolution. The

United States, too, has not shunned violent means to rid itself of hated opposition — an obvious example was our own Revolution. Less open, however, are efforts to bring down a government in another country because that government poses a threat to our own security or simply because leaders in our country may feel a particular form of government is harmful or evil. The United States, over the last few years, has helped its allies in Vietnam, in Korea, and in Central America. Sometimes, it does this by sending money to buy weapons, at other times, by sending in American troops to fight, or advise the country's armed forces. And while the United States has never engaged in wholesale terrorism as do some other nations, it has, nonetheless, been linked, through its Central Intelligence Agency, to plots on the lives of several political leaders in other countries.

The United States, of course, is not alone in such activities. Today, the Soviet Union does exactly as we do — and in the past, worse. During the repressive era of Joseph Stalin, the Soviets made widespread use of terrorism and execution to solidify their position. Soviet secret police — known variously as the Cheka, GPU, OGPU, NKVD, MGB, and now the KGB — were no better than Hitler's Gestapo, or secret state police, one of the sinister organizations the Germans used to terrorize citizens who opposed the Nazi government. Both the Gestapo and the KGB killed and tortured countless people, and imprisoned thousands of dissidents. In the case of the Nazis, their widespread concentration-camp system was used to exterminate some four million Jews.

Today, a glance at the headlines or at television will

tell you that government-sponsored violence has not disappeared: in Iran, the government of the fanatical Ayatollah Ruhollah Khomeini executes by firing squad former officials of the deposed Shah and political and religious opponents; in Suriname, on the northern coast of South America, fifteen prominent men — including lawyers, journalists, and a professor — are taken from their beds by military policemen for plotting to overthrow the government and are shot to death, the official explanation being that they were trying to escape; in Zimbabwe, in Africa, hundreds of civilians are summarily executed by government troops in violation of all internationally accepted standards of justice; in El Salvador, violence has become the leading cause of death as the government battles leftist guerrillas, tortures political prisoners, and kills and imprisons health workers. In a statement that could well apply wherever government-backed violence flourishes, a delegation that recently visited El Salvador commented, "Human rights infractions run so deep that there is an overall debasement of human life."[10]

Terrorism operates, of course, even without government sponsorship. Today, there are many organized bands of political terrorists who represent "shadow governments," governments, in effect, without a country, or without control within a country. Many of their names and initials have become household words: the Irish Republican Army (IRA), the Palestine Liberation Organization (PLO), the Italian Red Brigades, the Puerto Rican independence group known as Fuerzas Armadas de Liberación Nacional (FALN). Others in today's news are not so familiar, such as the Tamil Liberation Tigers, who seek independence from the government of Sri Lanka, and Armed Proletarian Power, an Italian group dedicated to wiping out prison staff. Highly visible or not, they all exist to force change, to call attention to their group's cause, or to avenge a real or imagined or long-past insult or wrong. To accomplish these goals, they may bomb public buildings, kill policemen, assassinate political leaders, hijack commercial planes, take hostages, and injure or massacre the innocent as well as those they have found guilty. According to the U.S. State Department, there were 746 cases of terrorist incidents in the world in 1982, 37 more than in the previous year; in all, 126 people were killed and 741 wounded.[11]

Always, the violence that accompanies a terrorist action is dramatic — a block-shaking bomb blast calls infinitely more attention to a cause than a drop of poison placed in an enemy's wineglass. And it is usually quite loathsome. In May of 1972, for instance, three members of the terrorist Japanese United Red Army opened fire with automatic rifles on unsuspecting waiting passengers at Israel's Lod Airport; they also heaved hand grenades into the panicked crowd. In a few seconds, more than twenty innocent people had been killed and nearly eighty wounded. As often happens in such situations, the terrorists themselves did not escape: one was killed accidentally by his comrades, another slipped on the bloody floor and died when a hand grenade went off before he could throw it, and the third was captured and sentenced to life in prison. In explaining why he and his fellow terrorists committed such a horrid crime, the surviving terrorist ranted, "I warn the entire world. The Red Army will slay anyone who is on the side of the bourgeois. Revolutionary warfare must be worldwide. In New York and Washington, the houses of simple people will be destroyed, so that they will feel the sweeping torrent of world revolution. We know this. We know that our struggle will become more severe than warfare between nations, but this too is inevitable."[12]

A few months after the Lod attack, Palestinian guerrillas murdered nine Israeli hostages at the Olympic Games in Munich, and not long after that, some thirty passengers were slaughtered in a grounded jet plane in Rome.

Sometimes, terrorism is directed at a single person who symbolizes a political philosophy or form of government the terrorists hate. In 1978, for instance, former Italian Prime Minister Aldo Moro was kidnapped in Rome by the Red Brigades, held hostage, then murdered. In that case, members of the gang were rounded up and thirty-two were convicted and sentenced to life in prison for the murder and for other crimes.

While the methods and weapons used by such groups may be new, their spiritual heritage, if one can use a word that often relates to sacred matters, stretches back at least to the days of the murderous Persian (Persia is now known as Iran) Hasan ibn-al-Sabbah (1007–1091); the hundreds of political murders this madman directed in the Middle East won him the title of First Grand Master of the Order of Assassins. His feared organization's sinister name came from its members' ritual use of the drug hashish, and the popular Arabic name for hashish smokers, *hashshāshin,* is the root of our word, assassin. (The crusaders, soldier-Christians who battled the Muslims for control of the Holy Land, used the word *assassin* to mean political murder.)

From a high mountain fortress, ibn-al-Sabbah directed a ruthless campaign against the overlords of other sects in Persia, Iraq, and Syria. With poison and dagger as their means of dealing death to carefully selected victims, the Assassins struck terror wherever they appeared. To win and keep their devotion to him, ibn-al-Sabbah played on their gullibility and their cultural and religious traditions. Here is how one writer has described the way the leader of the Assassins indoctrinated his men:

He constructed a secret garden and furnished it with all the delights promised in the Koran [the Muslim counterpart of the Bible] to the faithful when they reached paradise. The chosen were drugged, one or two at a time, and taken to this garden by night. When they woke up in the morning they were surrounded by beautiful and scantily clad houris [in Muslim belief, women who live with the blessed in paradise] who would minister to their every need and desire. After being allowed to savor this false — but pleasant and sensual — paradise for a day or so, they were again drugged before being taken back to awaken in their own squalid hovel or cave dwelling. To them, it was as if it had been a vivid dream. Ben Sabbah then sent for them, told them Allah had given them a preview of paradise, and surprised them by telling them exactly what each had been up to while in the secret garden. So successful was he in this method of conditioning and indoctrination that it was said he once astounded a visiting emir whom he wanted to impress with his power by sending for one of his men and ordering him to kill himself — which he immediately did.[13]

When an Assassin was sent out by ibn-al-Sabbah to carry out some violent deed, the Assassin was just as dedicated. So convinced were the Assassins that they would be rewarded in paradise that they never hesitated to fulfill their missions of murder, even though this often meant that their victims' bodyguards would kill them immediately afterward.

Such fanaticism is still a key ingredient in welding together terrorist organizations. Without the members' blind willingness to sacrifice their lives for the group's cause, without such narrow-minded devotion to an idea, no terrorist group can exist for long. Everyone has heard of skyjackers who threaten to blow up a plane, including themselves, if their demands are not met, or of terrorists who barricade themselves in a building with hostages and exchange gunfire with police, knowing full well that none inside the building is likely to survive.

But self-sacrifice like that is not peculiar to terrorist organizations of the kind we have been discussing. During World War II, Japanese pilots, known as kamikazes (divine wind), aimed their explosive-laden single-seat planes into U.S. warships in suicide missions. Wrote one member of a kamikaze squadron before his takeoff: "Still obeying my mother's instructions, I am about to scatter myself over an enemy ship. I am now going to make my long hoped for sortie to protect our Emperor, with a happy smile over being born a Japanese boy. Wishing for eternal peace and prosperity for Imperial Japan, I will bloom as a cherry blossom at Yasukuni Shrine." Sometimes, that kind of fanaticism spread to the pilots' families. "My son left our home when the cherry blossoms on yonder mountain burst into full bloom, telling us he would strike like a thunderbolt with his plane," one father wrote proudly.[14]

Political terrorists and wartime fanatics are not the only ones who band together and use violence to force an issue or gain some advantage. Religious fanatics, too, have done so. Indeed, the word *thug,* which is used to describe any brutal ruffian, originally referred to a worshiper of the Hindu goddess of death and destruction, Kali. Thugs practiced *thuggee,* the strangling of human victims as sacrifices to the frightful black, blood-smeared, four-armed idol that represented Kali. The Zealots, a Jewish sect active in the first century A.D., were another group that resorted to brutality, although for different reasons than the Thugs. Zealots were fervent observers of Jewish law — our word *zealous* is derived from their name, and it means fanatical devotion — who also fiercely opposed the Roman domination of Palestine. On the one hand, the Zealots are admired, even today, for a heroic last stand they made against Roman legions from a great rock named Masada at the edge of the Judaean desert; in a dramatic instance of violence turned inward, most of the Zealots committed suicide rather than surrender. But, the Zealots have also been denounced for engaging in lawless violence against the Romans, assassinating many of them along with their Jewish supporters.

Centuries later, the Roman Catholic church had its Inquisition, a tribunal organized to ferret out and punish heresy — the holding of opinions contrary to church dogma — and other offenses against the faith. In the early days of the church, heretics were usually punished by excommunication, but by the twelfth and thirteenth centuries, stirred by the growth of sects that expressed undoctrinal ideas, the church began to seek the aid of the state in suppressing such thinking. Emperor Frederick II of the Holy Roman Empire instituted the Inquisition in 1232, entrusting the search for heretics to state officials. Pope Gregory IX joined in, appointing inquisitors from the Dominican and Franciscan religious orders to uphold the church's authority in the matters under investigation. Suspects were arrested at night, held in tiny underground dungeons, and brought before secret courts in local monasteries; torture, authorized by Pope Innocent IV in 1252, was used to break their will. The torturers wore long black gowns, and hoods with holes for the eyes, mouth, and nose. Typically, a prisoner's arms were tied behind him with one end of a long rope; when the other end of the rope was pulled up over a rafter, the prisoner's arms were painfully dislocated. Or, a cloth would be used to cover a prisoner's mouth and nose, and water poured over his face; sometimes, lard was rubbed on the soles of the feet and a flame applied. Obstinate heretics were handed over to secular authorities for punishment — which usually meant death by burning at the stake.

It is interesting to note that the reason heretics were usually burned was that the Inquisition was forbidden to "shed blood" — which would have gone against a Catholic axiom that stated, *Ecclesia non vivit sanguinem* (The Church is untainted with blood). But tainted the church was, nevertheless, and no one contributed more to that reputation than the grand inquisitor, Tomás de Torquemada (1420–1498), a Dominican who led the notorious Spanish Inquisition. Known for his wanton cruelty, Torquemada was responsible for the deaths of some two thousand heretics. In 1875, writer Charles William Heckethorn, an authority on secret societies, had this to say about Torquemada and his inquisition:

He was so abhorred that he never stirred abroad without being surrounded by 250 familiars, and on his table always lay a horn of the unicorn, which according to Moorish superstition, was supposed to possess the virtue of discovering and nullifying the force of poison. His cruelties excited so many complaints that the Pope [Sixtus IV] himself was startled, and three times Torquemada was obliged to justify his conduct. During the fifteenth century so many executions took place at Seville that the prefect of that city had the diabolical idea, in order to expedite the process, to erect, outside the city, a permanent scaffold in stone, on which he placed four gigantic statues in plaster, hollow inside, into which New Christians, accused of having relapsed into their old faith, were forced, and slowly calcined [roasted] to death, as in a kiln. This scaffold was called *quemadero* [the burner], and the ruins of it could be seen as late as the year 1823.[15]

Even those who escaped death or lifelong imprisonment — only about one out of every two thousand accused — were not let off lightly. Again, Heckethorn:

The most fortunate, those that were reconciled, had to appear, bareheaded, with a cord around their necks, clothed in the *san benito,* an ugly garment, something like a sack, with black and yellow or white stripes and carrying a green wax taper in their hands, in the hall of the tribunal, or sometimes in a church, where, on their knees, they abjured the heresies laid to their charge. They were then condemned to wear the ignominious garment for some considerable time. Several other degrading and troublesome conditions were imposed on them, and the greater portion or whole of their property was confiscated; this was the rule the holy fathers never departed from. The *relaxed,* or those condemned to death, dressed in an even more hideous garb than the reconciled, having the portrait of the victim immersed in flames, and devils dancing about it, painted on thereon, were led out to the place of execution, attended by monks and friars, and burnt at the stake.[16]

Today, of course, the Catholic church condemns the Inquisition for its methods and misuse of power, but few critical voices were raised during the Middle Ages, so caught up were church officials in justifying their ends with extreme means.

Another church-connected group that operated in secrecy and used violence was the Danites. It was founded in Missouri in 1838, allegedly by authority of the Mormon church. Also known as the Avenging Angels, the Daughters of Zion, Big Fan, and the Daughters of Gideon, the group was bound by oath under penalty of death, and figured prominently in Sir Arthur Conan Doyle's first Sherlock Holmes novel, *A Study in Scarlet*. The society was apparently formed to defend the Mormons from their enemies, but many crimes were later attributed to its members; among these were the reprisal burnings of property of non-Mormons, and the massacre of a party of 140 non-Mormons from Arkansas and Missouri while they were on their way by wagon to southern California. For this crime, the Mormon bishop John D. Lee was convicted and executed by the federal government. Mormons generally either disavow any connection with the Danites, or they deny that the group existed.

The Danites and the Inquisition were linked to specific churches, directing their violence at nonmembers, or members who did not adhere to established beliefs. Even today, religion-associated violence erupts on occasion, as in India in 1983, when hundreds of Moslems and Hindus were killed in serious outbreaks that had religious, ethnic, and political overtones. But other groups, not tied to any religion, have also turned against members of various faiths. Quite often, these groups have included race along with religion as a target for violent acts. In the mid-1850s, for example, the Native American party was formed to prevent Roman Catholics and foreigners from winning public office. Originally a secret society, it was popularly called the Know-Nothing party because when its members were asked questions about what they stood for they replied, "I know nothing." The Know-Nothings assaulted immigrants and Catholics on the streets and in their homes, taking several lives before the organization finally faded away.

But the Know-Nothings were an amateurish footnote in history compared with the members of a feared organization that is still with us today — the Ku Klux Klan. Founded in 1866 at Pulaski, Tennessee, as a social club, the KKK (Ku Klux Klan is the corruption of a Greek word, *kuklos,* meaning "circle") degenerated into a misguided band of bigots that left a trail of death, destruction, and burning crosses — its symbol — in the name of Protestant white supremacy. Anti-Jew, anti-Catholic and anti-black, the Klansmen, clad in white hooded robes and using pompous titles like Grand Dragon, Great Cyclops, Grand Wizard of the Empire, Grand Titan of the Dominion, and Most Worshipful Turk, claimed 2.5 million members in 1924; most of them were in the South and Middle West. Politically powerful for many years, the Klan was able during its heyday to elect public officials, ruin those who opposed it, and enact legislation favorable to its biased beliefs. The words of a Georgia anti-KKK law of 1868 describe the Klan best: "A secret organization of men who, under the cover of masks and other grotesque disguises, armed with knives, revolvers and other deadly weapons, do issue from the place of their rendezvous . . . generally in the late hours of the night, to commit violence and outrage upon peaceable and law-abiding citizens, robbing and murdering them upon the highways, and entering their houses, tearing them from their homes and the embrace of their families, and, with violent threats and insults, inflicting upon them the most cruel and inhuman treatment . . . disturbing the public peace, ruining the happiness and property of the people, and in many places over-riding the civil authorities, defying all law and justice."[17]

Klan orders were frequently announced with mysterious public notices tacked up in conspicuous places, like this one:

DUNBAR'S SEPULCHRE, BLOODY MONTH
CLOUDY MOON, LAST HOUR

SPECIAL ORDER NO. 2

SHROUDED BROTHERS OF FORT DONELSON,
DIVISION NO. 51

The Great Past Grand Knight commands you. The dark and dismal hour draws nigh. Some live today, tomorrow die. The Whetted Sword, the Blade, the bullet Red and the Right are ours. Be Vigilant today. Mark well our friends. Let the guilty beware.

BY ORDER OF THE GREAT GRAND CYCLOPS[18]

Efforts to stop the Klan were initially unsuccessful because many law-enforcement officials were themselves members of the organization, or were at least sympathetic to its teachings. Sometimes, because

Klansmen sat on juries, accused members of the organization were easily acquitted. "It made its name a symbol of terror and desperation," observed one writer. "There are many thousands of Americans who think of it as an indefensible gang of outlaws and murderers. But ask any person who lived in the South during that wild nightmare called the Reconstruction and who saw the Klansmen as they went about their self-appointed task, ask such a one and from the light in his eyes it will be easy to see that the Klan in his memory is clad in shining armor, *sans peur et sans reproche.*"[19]

But the knights in dubious shining armor eventually rode for a fall. In 1871, President Ulysses S. Grant was given congressional authority to call out troops to restore order in Klan areas; the move was successful, and the KKK virtually disappeared.

In 1915, the Klan was revived again, in Atlanta, Georgia, with a stronger philosophy that placed the organization against everything, it seemed, except America, Mother, and Apple Pie. Once again, the KKK rode through the night, acting as a vigilante group, taking the law into its own hands to punish those it deemed to be un-American and immoral. Its influence eventually waned, revived briefly just before World War II, and again during the civil rights movement in the South in the 1960s. Today, the KKK is a small group of extremists with little sympathy outside its ranks. There are occasional episodes of alleged violence, as occurred in 1979 when five members of the Communist Workers party were slain in Greensboro, North Carolina. A group of six Klansmen and Nazi party members were tried for the crime, but were acquitted the following year.

When the Klan is heard from nowadays, it is usually at a relatively peaceful rally, kept that way by hordes of policemen who are on hand to protect the group's First Amendment rights. Chances are the Klansmen wear white robes, but usually without hoods, and their speeches generally focus on opposition to forced busing to achieve racial integration in schools, and on what is called reverse discrimination, that is, discrimination against whites.

These rather mild activities are a far cry from what the Ku Klux Klan stood for during the height of its activities. That mellowing with age is, unfortunately, not the case with what we know as organized crime, an activity that stretches back many years and is perhaps more powerful and more extensive than it ever was. Understand, however, that we are not talking about the youthful street gangs that have long terrorized urban areas, gangs whose members rob, murder, and rape, and who wear their own insignia on jackets, or paint them on walls of their tenement headquarters. With fear-inspiring names like Black Devils, Satan's Brood, Savage Angels, and Death's Doors, they are the latest and most violent in a long line of street criminals that make the pickpockets and thieves hired by the villainous Fagin of Charles Dickens's *Oliver Twist* seem like a Sunday school troop. These groups, often formed to give status and identity to youths who have neither, have been known to offer their services to drug dealers, acting as protectors, collecting debts, and intimidating witnesses. But such gangs are not part of any closely knit nationwide organization with a common goal.

When we speak of organized crime, we are referring to what is commonly called the underworld, a social sphere of criminals that operates far below the level of ordinary life. It is a formidable enterprise that siphons off millions upon millions of dollars in illegal profits every year and is, truly, the most noteworthy of the violence-ridden organizations we have been discussing.

Organized crime operates like any well-run industry, employing, as does a factory or office, accountants, lawyers, consultants, and business managers. It has its bosses to maintain order, underbosses to collect information for the bosses and pass instructions on to underlings, and advisers, who are usually retired, older members of the organization. It also has the support, in many instances, of corrupt law-enforcement officials and politicians on all levels, from small towns to the nation's capital. But the way it works and its goals are far different from those of legitimate businesses. Here is how a U.S. government task force report describes the underworld: "Organized crime is a society that seeks to operate outside the control of the American people and their government. It involves thousands of criminals, working within structures as complex as those of any large corporation, subject to laws more rigidly enforced than those of legitimate governments. Its actions are not impulsive but rather the result of intricate conspiracies, carried on over many years and aimed at gaining control over whole fields of activity in order to amass huge profits.

The core of organized crime activity is the supplying of illegal goods and services — gambling, loan-sharking (lending money at exorbitant interest rates), narcotics and other forms of vice — to countless numbers of citizen customers. But organized crime is also extensively and deeply involved in legitimate business and in labor unions. Here it employs illegitimate methods — monopolization, terrorism, extortion, tax evasion — to drive out or control lawful ownership and leadership and to exact illegal profits from the public. And to carry on its many activities secure from governmental interference, organized crime corrupts public officials. . . .

What organized crime wants is money and power. What makes it different from law-abiding organizations and individuals with those same objectives is that the ethical and moral standards the criminals adhere to, the laws and regulations they obey, the procedures they use are private and secret ones that they devise themselves, change when they see fit, and administer summarily and invisibly. Organized crime affects the lives of millions of Americans, but because it desperately preserves its invisibility many, perhaps most, Americans are not aware how they are affected, or even that they are affected at all. The price of a loaf of bread may go up one cent as the result of an organized crime conspiracy, but a housewife has no way of knowing why she is paying more. If organized criminals paid income tax on every cent of their vast earnings, everybody's tax bill would go down, but no one knows how much.[20]

Organized crime's activities and its members have been highly publicized in the news media; there have been movies and books, such as *The Godfather;* and the name of one large criminal group — Mafia, also known as La Cosa Nostra or the Mob — has become a household word. According to law-enforcement officials, the Mafia is made up of criminal cartels operating in large cities across the nation. Membership generally consists of men of Italian descent who are, according to authorities, in frequent communication with one another, and whose overall activities are guided by a national board of overseers. Other ethnic groups, of course, have long banded together for criminal purposes: Chinese tongs, for instance, preyed on the Oriental communities in New York and San Francisco for many years, controlling drug trade and gambling and engaging in frequent bloody gang wars. The name Mafia, in fact, is often used to mean an organization of criminals no matter what their ethnic background. Gangs of Irish-American crooks are known as the Irish Mafia, and in the South, law officers now refer, for want of a better name, to the Dixie Mafia, a loose alliance of drug smugglers, killers for hire, car thieves, and operators of prostitution and pornography rings. This group apparently has no connection to the tightly structured Mafia, and is made up of ruthless men and women of various ethnic origins.

The Mafia itself (used interchangeably here with La Cosa Nostra, which means "Our Thing" or "Our Affair" in Italian) got its start as a secret criminal organization many years ago on the island of Sicily. The word is apparently derived from an Arabic one meaning a place of refuge — as a result of the Arab conquest of the island in the ninth century, many Sicilians founded "mafias" in the hills, using them as hideouts when they eventually turned into peasant bandits. During the nineteenth century, the organization increased its power, dominating politics, offering "protection" to merchants by blackmail, and terrorizing the countryside. Its members were bound by a code of honor and silence called *omertà*, which meant that a Mafioso, as a member was called, was not to give evidence before the courts, or seek any help from them.

Sicilian immigrants to the United States introduced the Mafia here, where it became a growing nuisance in the late 1800s. In one celebrated case during that period, Joseph Petrosino, a New York City detective who had been born in Italy, was assigned to investigate the activities of the Mafia and another secret society called the Black Hand. Petrosino decided to broaden his investigation by going to Sicily, and while there, he was murdered by two men who fired their pistols into his head as he was on his way to the police headquarters. The murder was never solved.

That sort of violence, as most everyone now knows, has become the hallmark of organized crime groups like the Mafia. As that organization sought to consolidate its power, hundreds of gangsters were murdered, many of them during the Prohibition period. This began officially on January 16, 1920, when the Volstead Act, passed earlier by Congress, enforced the Eighteenth Amendment to the Constitution, making the entire United States "dry." This meant that bars, package stores, and breweries would be closed, and no one would be able to buy whiskey, wine, or beer — that is, not legally. People who wanted a drink could still buy one at illegally run speakeasies, which were nightclubs and bars known to just about everyone, including the police; or, liquor could be purchased from neighborhood dealers who made their own moonshine or bathtub gin at home and sold it for a dollar a bottle.

But not all the illegal liquor was made by friendly, local entrepreneurs. Much of it was smuggled into the country from outside, where it was legal, either by fast motorboats from islands in the Caribbean, or in trucks coming across the border from Canada. Most of this liquor was sold in the speakeasies, and inevitably both supplying and selling it came under the control of organized crime. Bootlegging, as the outlawed liquor industry came to be known, was big business — putting millions of dollars a day into the pockets of racketeers and corrupt public officials. With bootlegging came a wave of underworld violence the likes of which the United States has not seen since. In Chicago alone, there were 765 gangland murders between 1920 and 1934, an average of 48 a year. Among the notable gangsters of the time was Alphonse (Scarface) Capone, a ruthless man of Sicilian origin who controlled racketeering in Chicago through strong organization and by killing rival gangsters. After the celebrated Saint Valentine's Day Massacre of 1929 — in which seven rival gang leaders were machine-gunned to death — Capone was left in supreme control of the protection rackets, speakeasies, and brothels.

Today, the Mafia in the United States still resorts to violence, although nowhere on the scale that it did back in the twenties. As Mark H. Furstenberg of the International Association of Chiefs of Police has pointed out, as organized crime has broadened its bases and increased its controls, it has become steadily less violent. "It is true that during its period of rapid change and development," he has observed, "when it was consolidating its strength, organized crime was violent, sometimes wildly so. But being far more inherently rational than they are inherently violent, organized crime's leaders, when they finally realized that of all their activities only violence exposed them to public criticism and law enforcement pressure, began to avoid violence, and to win a security which killing threatened. They developed and refined a system of rational alternatives to violence."[21]

But even though today's Mafia member may lead a less exciting and less violent life than the Mafioso of yesterday, or may not live up to the media's popular image of him, he is, nonetheless, still responsible indirectly for much violence. Because maintaining a heroin habit can cost more than a hundred dollars a day, the addict, who generally does not earn that kind of money, must steal it. Violent street crime, therefore, is committed to pay for the illegal drugs that organized crime controls. Organized criminal activity also contributes to perpetuating crime through the idolization of the mobster. "To ghetto youth, who see rich lords, well dressed and driving big cars, success comes to mean successful criminal activity, and the 'smart ones' are those who succeed in the mob," says Furstenberg.[22]

The government task force report points to the case

of Frank Costello of New York City, a man who had been repeatedly called a leader of organized crime, as an example of the subtle way organized crime has an impact on our lives. Costello lived in an expensive Central Park apartment, was often seen dining in famous restaurants in the company of judges, public officials, and prominent businessmen. He was shaved every morning in the barbershop of the plush Waldorf-Astoria Hotel. He played golf on weekends at a country club on the fashionable north shore of Long Island. "In short, though his reputation was common knowledge," said the report, "he moved around New York conspicuously and unashamedly, perhaps ostracized by some people but more often accepted, greeted by journalists, recognized by children, accorded all the freedoms of a prosperous and successful man."[23] It is no wonder that the public is confused. Faced with constant reminders that criminals — even those with a reputation for committing incredible violence — can be treated like pillars of the community, we often become indifferent; and we reason that if an organized crime kingpin can continually beat the system and stay out of jail, then our own relatively minor crimes are okay. Sometimes, though, those minor crimes escalate into offenses that are more serious, and in this way, what organized crime does also affects us indirectly.

It is important, then, to try to see behind the movie images of violent heroes, behind the benevolent poses that many criminals adopt by, say, giving large sums of money to churches, or by becoming community leaders. The recent remarks of Pope John Paul II, spoken in Palermo, Sicily, heartland of the Italian Mafia, got to the core of the matter: "Facts of barbarous violence, which for too long a time have bloodied the streets of this splendid city, offend human dignity."[24] His remarks were appropriate: the Mafia was behind more than a hundred murders and another hundred or so disappearances in 1982, along with more than two hundred fifty deaths the same year in Naples, on the Italian mainland.

There is another important thing to remember when considering some of the examples of group violence we have outlined. That is, that it would be unfair to suspect all members of a religious, ethnic, or political organization just because some have adopted violence as a handmaiden. The Mormon Danites are a thing of the past, and they were but a handful of individuals from a respected church. Hitler's Gestapo and the American KKK should not be linked, even in jest, to Germans and southerners, respectively, of today. Not all Palestinians are terrorists, nor all Irish, nor all the people of Puerto Rico, nor all striking union workers. Even in countries where violent methods are employed to coerce people, one cannot condemn everyone who lives in those countries, or associate them with the actions of those who govern them.

The case of the Mafia is an important one to consider. Because of the enormous publicity it has received in the United States and abroad, it has become associated with virtually every criminal act committed just about everywhere on earth. Given the incredible diversity of criminal activities in this world, such is obviously not true. For one thing, there is a strong difference of opinion over whether the Mafia that began in Sicily is the same one that dominates organized crime in America. True, many of its members are of Italian origin (but not all are of Sicilian origin), and the structure of the crime "families" closely parallels that of their overseas counterparts. But the fact is, many men of other ethnic groups work for what is called the Mafia in the United States; moreover, those who do have Italian backgrounds are most often American-born, and are not so tied to the old Italian traditions. Some do, of course, adhere to the old ways, but even many of those men do it to perpetuate the belief in, and the fear of, the Mafia as a powerful organization that has for centuries withstood all efforts to break it up. Even the current name, La Cosa Nostra, is fairly meaningless when describing organized crime. "The phrase incorrectly implies that all members of the conspiracy are Italian or Sicilian," sociologist Donald R. Cressey of the University of California at Santa Barbara remarked in the government task force report. "Further, the term is unknown outside New York [and] not even widely known in New York."[25]

Professor Cressey noted that one of the nation's foremost authorities on organized crime, Sergeant Ralph Salerno of the New York City Police Department, had been processing crime cases for many years, had listened to hundreds of conversations between Italian and Sicilian criminals, and interviewed dozens of informers. Perhaps only three times, said Cressey, did Salerno ever hear the words *Cosa Nostra* used to refer to the organization. One criminal might say to another,

Questa e una cosa nostra, which means, "This is an affair of ours." It does not mean, "I am a member of 'Our Thing' or of 'Our Affair.' "

But labels are important to some people, especially to law-enforcement officials who need to fix blame on someone specific if only to appear to be doing their jobs properly; some members of the news media also tend to seize on a tag line and reproduce it over and over again until it sticks. And since it is usually easier to lay the blame on some influence — be it country of origin or a brain chemical gone wrong or an inherited defect — rather than on own's own backyard, meaning conditions in America, "Mafia" and "La Cosa Nostra" have become common expressions. But with them have come the myths and misconceptions that have, many times, done a disservice to Americans with Italian names. "It's run by the Mafia" is a popular expression one usually hears whispered across a restaurant table by someone who allegedly knows all about it. And unfortunately, if there is an Italian-American in the dinner party, he or she may smile enigmatically, not because the statement is true but perhaps because such a wicked connection is the source of some pride, misguided though it may be. Says Professor Cressey:

> It is a fact that the great majority, by far, of Italian and Sicilian immigrants and their descendants have been both fine and law-abiding citizens. They have somehow let criminals who are Italians or Sicilians, or Americans of Italian or Sicilian descent, be identified with them. Criminals of Italian or Sicilian descent are called "Italians" or "Sicilians" while bankers, lawyers and professors of Ital-

ian or Sicilian descent are called "Americans." Most Americans know the name "Luciano" [Charles "Lucky" Luciano was a crime boss in New York City] than know the name "Fermi" [Enrico Fermi, who won a Nobel Prize for studies in nuclear physics]. If the criminal cartel or confederation is an importation from Sicily and Italy, it should be disowned by all Italian-Americans and Sicilian-Americans because it does not represent the real cultural contribution of Italy and Sicily to America. If it is an American innovation, the men of Italian and Sicilian descent who have positions in it should be disowned by the respectable Italian-American and Sicilian-American community on the ground that they are participating in an extremely undesirable aspect of American culture.[26]

While the common ethnic tie of several thousand men who belong to organized crime's various groups cannot be ignored, it ought to be put into proper perspective. Perhaps Sergeant Palermo put it best when an Italian-American racketeer complained that one of his "own kind" — meaning Salerno, who is of Italian background — was hurting him. Replied the policeman, "I'm not your kind, and you're not my kind. My manners, morals, and mores are not yours. The only thing we have in common is that we both spring from an Italian heritage and culture — and you are a traitor to that heritage and culture which I am proud to be part of."[27]

In concluding this discussion of group violence, we cannot ignore the fact that groups of people sometimes direct their violent behavior not at someone else but at themselves. We have already mentioned the mass suicide of the Zealots at Masada, and the fanatical dive-bombing attacks on American warships (although these were aimed at others) by Japanese kamikaze pilots. Other similar incidents have caused the loss of many lives. In 1944, for example, some three thousand Japanese soldiers on the island of Saipan, most of them armed with nothing but bayonets and sticks, charged madly into a barrage of machine-gun fire from American marines, and were killed to the last man. Among those mowed down were previously wounded soldiers, bandaged and supported by their comrades, who had staggered out of field hospitals to participate in the suicide attack. The suicides were not limited to soldiers. As U.S. troops ranged over the island they saw evidence of mass suicide among the civilian population. In probably the saddest incident of all, hundreds of Japanese civilians — many of them women with babies in their arms — threw themselves off cliffs into the sea, rather than suffer the disgrace of being captured. According to one account, the self-slaughter continued for three days, and when the island was finally quiet, fewer than one thousand Japanese survived out of the original thirty-two thousand occupants.

Finally, in 1978, in a horrifying scene in the Guyana jungle of South America, some nine hundred followers of the People's Temple, a San Francisco–based religious cult led by the Reverend Jim Jones, killed themselves or were killed by other cult members, by drinking a soft drink spiked with poison. Jones's body, with a bullet in the head, was found near an altar in the camp. Just prior to the mass suicides, U.S. Representative Leo

J. Ryan of California, who had been investigating complaints that cult members were being mistreated, was shot dead with four others in an airport ambush as they tried to leave Guyana with some cult members who wanted to flee to the United States. It was a tragic end to a tale that stands as a monumental example of group violence, of humanity run amok.

·3·

ASSASSINATION

Assassination is the extreme form of censorship.

— GEORGE BERNARD SHAW

JUST BEFORE HE PARTICIPATES in the assassination of Julius Caesar, Brutus gives his fellow conspirators this bit of advice: "Let's kill him boldly, but not wrathfully. Let's carve him as a dish fit for the gods, not hew him as a carcass fit for hounds." Poetic though those words may be, they do not hide the simple fact that men had gathered to plan a murder to rid the Roman Empire of someone they did not like.

The killing of Julius Caesar was a political assassination, and there have been many others like it. Assassination, which usually refers to the sudden killing of a politically important person either by a hired murderer or by a fanatic, is all too familiar to Americans. But political officeholders have not been the only targets of deadly attack. Civil rights leaders, entertainers, lawyers, police officials, corporate executives, sports figures — all have come under fire or had their lives threatened. These victims and targets share a common bond that differentiates them from the victims of run-of-the-mill murders and murder attempts: each is in the public eye. And unfortunately, the more prominent the individual, the better the chance that he or she will become a target.

The office of President of the United States is a good example of how power and prestige can mark a man for violent death. According to a U.S. government report on assassination and political violence, one out of 4 Presidents has been a target for assassination, compared to approximately one out of every 166 governors, one out of 142 U.S. senators, and one out of every 1,000 congressmen. "We can suggest that the correlation between the importance of elected office and the likelihood of assassination is affected by the fact that the importance of the office and the size of the constituency are directly related," said the report. "The President's constituency is much larger than that of any other elected office. Similarly, a senator's or a governor's constituency is greater than that of any congressman."[1]

But even though the importance of an intended victim's political office determines his vulnerability, this does not mean — in the United States, at least — that the assassin wants to bring about some political change. This rarely occurs in our country. With the exception of attacks upon Republicans in the South during the Reconstruction era, in which the seceded states were reorganized after the Civil War, few of the deadly attacks against officeholders have been calculated to further the political aims of the assassin or of some organized effort to overthrow the government. Only a handful fit the classic picture of an assassination for a rational political purpose. In 1900, Governor William Goebel of Kentucky narrowly won a bitterly contested three-way fight for the governorship among his own Populist Democrats, conservative Democrats, and the incumbent Republicans. Three men associated with the Republican party were convicted of conspiracy to assassinate the governor. In 1935, Huey P. Long (known as "The Kingfish"), the senator from Louisiana, was murdered by Carl Weiss, a twenty-nine-year-old physician from a wealthy, professional family. Many commentators have suggested that Long was killed because Weiss was disturbed by the possibility that Long would make a bid for national power before the 1936 presidential election. In the eyes of many, Long was a demagogue, an extremely dangerous political figure.

But such deliberate political acts of assassination as the one directed at Huey Long are rare in our country. This lack of political motivation in attempts on an officeholder's life extends also to the presidency, in that presidential assassinations and attempts seem to be the work of men and women with deranged minds. Said Dr. Lawrence Z. Freedman, who developed a profile of presidential assassins for the Secret Service after the shooting of President Kennedy: "The assassins of American presidents have been emotionally disturbed social isolates, acting on their own, without any rational expectation that they, or the party and cause with which they are identified, could benefit from the slaying."[2]

It is hard to explain why a person assassinates or attempts to assassinate a President or any other public figure. Assassins and would-be assassins have come from every socioeconomic class, from various religious and ethnic groups. Certainly, many have the ability to conceive and execute a plan almost flawlessly, which says something about their general competence. As was noted in the discussion of the causes of violent behavior, many factors are at work in the mind and body of such a killer. Nevertheless, psychiatrists continue to look for similarities among the assassins, and though a definitive profile has yet to emerge — some of the characteristics fit many people who do not become assassins and who, in fact, lead very normal lives — some generalities may be observed. Many, for example, had no relationship with their parents, or a disrupted one. Most have been loners who had a difficult time making friends of either sex; in the case of the men (most have been males), most had difficulty establishing lasting relationships with women. Another common characteristic is the tendency to identify with a cause or some ideology, but the inability to participate with others in that cause. Most of the presidential assassins and would-be assassins felt no remorse; they believed that what they had done was justified. Many had a spotty work record just prior to the assassination.

Several of these characteristics fit the picture of what is known as a sociopathic personality; this is a disordered behavioral state in which a person is repeatedly in conflict with society, has no loyalty to others, is callous, irresponsible, impulsive, totally without guilt, and unwilling or unable to learn from others or from punishment; such a person also quite often blames others for his or her difficulties.

The following brief profiles of some of those who tried to kill U.S. Presidents, or who succeeded, will give a better understanding of the mind of an assassin.

RICHARD LAWRENCE

A native Englishman, Lawrence was in his early thirties when he tried to shoot Andrew Jackson, the seventh President, in the rotunda of the Capitol on January 30, 1835. Fortunately for Jackson, both pistols Lawrence held misfired.

Little is known about Lawrence's childhood beyond the fact that he was apparently a well-behaved child. Later, he became a house painter, and also painted landscapes as a hobby. He never married.

About two years before he tried to kill Jackson, Lawrence underwent a noticeable personality change. He became violent, and had delusions that he was King Richard III of England; he also began to believe that the U.S. government owed him large sums of money, and he began attending sessions of Congress to keep track of his claims. He also convinced himself that Jackson was preventing him from getting the money.

Lawrence was found innocent by reason of insanity, and he spent the rest of his life in mental institutions.

JOHN WILKES BOOTH

Son of the actor Junius Booth, John Wilkes Booth gained notoriety as the man who shot and killed Abraham Lincoln, the sixteenth President, on April 14, 1865, in Ford's Theater, Washington, D.C.

Booth was an unruly (and illegitimate) child; his father and brothers were often absent for long periods because of theatrical tours. He never finished high school, and was unable or unwilling to take to formal schooling of any kind. Although he seemed to have natural acting talent, he was undisciplined and never learned the craft properly. He had many women companions, traveled in southern social circles, and had a tendency to be moody and unpredictable.

About a year before the assassination, Booth's voice grew weak and hoarse, either the result of inadequate voice training, or the first signs of some emotional illness. His sympathies for the South began to deepen, and on one occasion he nearly strangled his own brother-in-law for making a disparaging remark about Jefferson Davis, president of the Confederacy. He also came to believe that Lincoln had been elected through vote fraud.

Booth, who claimed that he had done God's will in killing Lincoln, was cornered by Union soldiers in a barn some days after the assassination. He died from a bullet in the head, fired either by himself or by a soldier who said later that he did so as an agent of the Lord.

CHARLES J. GUITEAU

On July 2, 1881, in a Washington train station, Guiteau shot and fatally wounded James A. Garfield, four months after Garfield was sworn in as the nation's twentieth President. If there is such a thing as a textbook description of a presidential assassin, Guiteau fits it. His mother died when he was seven, and he was raised by his father, a deeply religious man. The Guiteau family had a history of mental illness: an uncle died insane, Charles's two sisters were probably insane, and his two first cousins were sent to asylums.

Charles became a Bible student, and later joined the Oneida Community in New York, a rather strange experiment in communal living and religion in which sex was encouraged but marriage avoided because it implied ownership. Later, Guiteau criticized the sexual permissiveness of the community and urged that it be criminally prosecuted.

He became a lawyer, but began cheating his clients out of money. He borrowed money and failed to pay it back, and ran out on boardinghouses before paying his bills. Guiteau married a sixteen-year-old girl, but later was divorced on grounds of his adultery. He eked out a living by publishing religious pamphlets, stealing most of his ideas but alleging that they came from God.

Guiteau eventually convinced himself that he deserved a high government position, and began pestering the White House for a job. At about this time, he decided that God wanted him to protect the country from Garfield, so he bought a pistol with borrowed money. He stalked the President, but decided against killing him on two occasions: once because Mrs. Garfield was present, and the second time because it was too hot and Guiteau was too tired. When he finally did it, he was methodical. Says the U.S. government's report on assassination, "On the day he finally determined to kill Garfield, Guiteau hired a hack to wait for him and take him immediately to jail lest the angry mobs harm him."[3]

Before he was hanged, Guiteau argued that he was innocent because he had acted on orders from God. He added, "I predict that this nation will go down in blood and that my murderers, from the executive to the hangman, will go to hell."[4]

LEON F. CZOLGOSZ

The man who fatally wounded William McKinley, the twenty-fifth President, on September 6, 1901, as the President was about to shake his hand at a reception in Buffalo, New York, was the son of Polish immigrants. Czolgosz's mother died when he was twelve, and he was known to be a shy, withdrawn child with no close friends. He has been described as obsessively neat and, interestingly, as someone who disliked cruelty; he even refused to kill insects.

A devout Catholic and a steady worker at a mill, Czolgosz eventually fell away from his church when he began to suspect that priests were misleading him. At about age twenty-two, he grew listless and a few years later suffered a nervous breakdown. He became suspicious of people, and, out of fear he would be poisoned, began eating food he prepared himself in his room.

He tried to join a group of anarchists, a political group that believed in no government whatsoever, but acted so strangely that the members thought he was a police informer. After he shot McKinley and was wrestled to the ground by onlookers, he reportedly told police, "My name is Fred Nieman, Fred Nobody. Nobody killed the President."

Remorseless to the very moment he was strapped into the electric chair, Czolgosz told his executioners, "I killed the President because he was the enemy of good people — the good working people. I am not sorry for my crime."

LEE HARVEY OSWALD

On November 22, 1963, Lee Harvey Oswald assassinated the nation's thirty-fifth President, John F. Kennedy, firing a rifle at him while the President and his wife and Texas Governor John Connally were passing in a motorcade in Dallas. Governor Connally was wounded in the attack.

There was little to be learned from Oswald about the murder because he himself was murdered shortly after the assassination by nightclub operator Jack Ruby in a sudden and violent act that was witnessed by millions of Americans on live television. But probably more is known about the Kennedy assassination and the assassin than any other, and the voluminous details are contained in the Report of the President's Commission on the Assassination of President Kennedy, also called the Warren Report.

Dr. Freedman, who has studied the personalities of presidential assassins, has said this of Oswald: "He was born two months after the death of his father to a mother who, as far as we can ascertain, was so preoccupied that she could spare little feeling for her son. She alternated between clinging to him and sending him elsewhere to live, warning him away from other children, and, at home, literally keeping him in her bed until he reached puberty. Oswald became a politically and personally alienated man, married but estranged from a wife who publicly ridiculed him for his inability to earn a living and for his sexual indifference."[5]

Oswald was a loner with few friends, and in his early years was diagnosed as being emotionally disturbed. He joined the marines, but was unable to take orders and got an early discharge. He went to Russia and tried to defect, but the Russians would not allow him to become a citizen. Unlike the other assassins mentioned here, Oswald denied that he had ever hurt anyone. However, witnesses saw him shoot a policeman that day in Dallas, and he was accused of shooting at an army general in an earlier assassination attempt.

Lynette ("Squeaky") Fromme

Fromme was a twenty-six-year-old follower of Charles Manson, the mass murderer convicted with three other female friends of the sadistic killing of actress Sharon Tate and six others in 1969.

On September 5, 1975, she was arrested by Secret Service agents as she pointed a loaded .45-caliber automatic at President Gerald Ford while he was shaking hands with a street crowd in Sacramento, California.

Fromme was the daughter of an aeronautical engineer; she dropped out of high school, joined Manson's "family," and became caught up in a world of drugs, sex, and obedience to Manson. After he was arrested, she and other followers remained on the courthouse steps during his trial; so devoted was she to Manson that she carved an *X* into her forehead to show loyalty, and shaved her head in protest. She was not implicated in the massacre that Manson led, but she was arrested many times for drug possession, and once for murder (she was acquitted of the latter charge). Of her, one Los Angeles detective commented, "The girl must have been on at least 1,000 acid [LSD] trips in her life. It was just not possible to hold a rational conversation with her."[6] Others commented that she often talked in praise of violence and killing.

Fromme insisted during her trial that she was not going to shoot the President, that she merely wanted to get attention for a new trial for Manson. The President himself testified at the trial, on videotape, to tell how he had been confronted by Fromme. "I saw a hand come through the crowd," he said. "In the hand there was a gun."[7]

Fromme's excuse was rejected by the jury, which found her guilty. She was sentenced to life in prison.

SARA JANE MOORE

Not long after "Squeaky" Fromme pointed her automatic at President Ford, Sara Jane Moore, forty-five, did the same thing, only this time a shot was fired. Moore shot at Ford on September 22, 1975, as the President was stepping out of a San Francisco hotel. The bullet struck the pavement after a bystander deflected the gun as Moore fired.

Moore came from a middle class West Virginia family, had been married three times, had wanted to be an actress, but later became increasingly active in radical groups. In one ironic twist, she also served briefly as an undercover informer for the FBI. "One thread seems to run consistently through all the twists and contradictions of Moore's story," said the *Washington Post* after the attempt on Ford's life. "She was, by almost all accounts, a woman of quickly shifting moods and bitter quarrels with friends and co-workers."[8]

According to psychiatrists, Moore had been hospitalized for mental treatment seven times in twenty-five years; one described her as "psychotic" and "out of contact with reality" when she was in a New York psychiatric hospital. Others said she had a tendency to boast of her "wealthy" southern background, and was always seeking attention.

Moore became an accountant, but did not hang on to her jobs for very long. Some of her former employers described her as too aggressive and difficult to get along with.

Moore was sentenced to life in prison by a judge who told her, "You wouldn't be standing before me now if we had an effective capital punishment law. The one thing that people care about is their skin." Moore also had something to say. In a ten-minute statement she asked herself whether she was sorry she had tried to kill Ford. Her answer was yes and no. "Yes," she said, "because it accomplished little except to throw away the rest of my life. And no, I'm not sorry I tried because at the time it seemed a correct expression of my anger . . . and if successful . . . just might have triggered the kind of chaos that could have started the upheaval of change."[9]

JOHN W. HINCKLEY, JR.

The twenty-six-year-old man who shot President Reagan and three others on March 30, 1981, in Washington, D.C., came from a well-to-do home. He was a loner and, according to his attorney, became increasingly withdrawn as he grew older, and began hiding in a fantasy world. He had dropped in and out of college, and had dreams of becoming a rock star. At one point, he became obsessed with the movie *Taxi Driver,* the story of a psychopathic character who stalked a presidential candidate. At the same time, he also became obsessed with Jodie Foster, an actress who co-starred in the film; Hinckley allegedly shot Reagan to win her admiration and affection. He also, according to a defense psychiatrist, felt jealousy and hatred toward the actress, and allegedly stalked her at Yale University, where she was a student. He apparently never bothered her but was said to have had a loaded gun in his pocket.

Said one psychiatrist, "He planned to accost her on campus and, depending on the outcome, he would either kill himself in front of her, or kill her and then himself."[10]

The troubled young man also visited the Dakota apartment building in New York City, where John Lennon was murdered, and stood with a pistol in his pocket on the spot where the former Beatle had died.

On June 21, 1982, Hinckley was found not guilty by reason of insanity, and was committed to a mental hospital for an indefinite period.

·4·

VIOLENCE IN SPORTS

> _He [man] is the only creature that inflicts_
> _pain for sport, knowing it to be pain._
>
> — MARK TWAIN

IN NOVEMBER OF 1982, a twenty-three-year-old South
Korean boxer, Duk Koo Kim, was badly beaten in a
professional title fight in Las Vegas. Taken from the
ring to the hospital by ambulance, the battered fighter
underwent nearly three hours of surgery during which
doctors removed a blood clot from the right side of his
brain. A broken blood vessel had caused the clot, which
was almost certainly the result, as the operating room
surgeon put it, of "one tremendous punch to the
head."[1]

Later, Kim's brain swelled from the terrible beating,
and he was kept "alive" for four days with a hospital
life-support machine. Doctors finally disconnected him
from the machine when it was obvious that Kim would
not be able to live on his own, and he died, one of more
than four hundred men fatally injured in boxing
matches since 1918. Said the fighter who beat him, Ray
"Boom Boom" Mancini, "I'm very saddened. I'm sorry

it had to happen, and it hurts me bad that I was part of it. I hope they realize I didn't intentionally hurt him. I don't blame myself, but I can't alienate myself."[2]

It is true, of course, that Mancini did not go into the ring to purposely cause his opponent's death. It is doubtful that any professional boxer does that. But it is also true that the goal of boxing is to win, either by gaining more points over one's opponent, or by hurting him so badly that he cannot continue. This often means knocking him unconscious. Once, the great champion Sugar Ray Robinson, who had caused the death of another fighter in a match, was asked if he knew he had his opponent in trouble. Robinson replied, "Sir, getting people in trouble is my business."[3]

The Kim-Mancini fight touched off a wave of protest against boxing. In an editorial, the *New York Times* questioned whether a civilized society can plausibly justify the pleasure it gains from a sport that causes visible and invisible damage. The newspaper answered:

> The Colosseum was packed when the Romans sent gladiators to fight to the death for sport. Holding that humans are more than meat, our age requires skill, not violence, to be the prime ability demonstrated in a sport. Boxing has progressed little from bare-knuckled butchery to Queensberry rules and gloves. Football may cause more injuries, mountaineering and auto racing may claim more lives, but boxing is the only sport in which the explicit goal is to injure the opponent. Even people offended by cockfighting and bullfighting somehow accept the deliberate maiming of the human body, perhaps because the worst damage appears after the blood has been wiped

away and the crowd has gone home sated. If boxers choose freely to fight, and the public to watch, why should others interfere? Because the public celebration of violence cannot be a private matter. And the boxers' choice is not so free. Adulation and promoters' greed impel some to return to the ring against their best interests. . The 21st century will surely appraise our coarseness of feeling with the same wonderment with which we contemplate the public hangings that were common in the 19th.[4]

The medical profession, too, was highly critical of the Kim-Mancini fight, and of boxing in general. A report in the *Journal of the American Medical Association* pointed out that in a study of thirty-eight former boxers, more than half showed signs of abnormal brain-tissue loss; there was also a clear connection between the number of times the man fought and the likelihood of his having such brain damage. "Boxing," said the report, "is the only sport in which the intent is to inflict physical injury. Particularly in professional boxing, the fighter who injures and ultimately causes his opponent to become helpless, earns, for some atavistic reason, the plaudits of the fans and therefore the highest monetary recompense."[5]

The same thing holds true in other sports in which violent behavior surfaces from time to time. We have come to expect violence in many of the games we watch. We all like tough players, men and women who are able to withstand and give out punishment when it has to be done. We also like winners, and sometimes, for many of us, it makes no difference how the game is won. If a

player is able to win a point because he is stronger —
and more aggressive even — than his opponent, then
we often reason that that is what the game is all about.
At a recent symposium on violence, held at the University of Toronto, Arnold Talentino, a literature teacher
at the State University of New York and someone with
an interest in sports violence, quoted Larry Zeidel, a
member of the 1975 Philadelphia Flyers hockey team,
as saying, "I needed every bit of toughness at my command. Toughness with the fist and toughness with the
stick because my opponents were ruthless. They'd put
their stick right through me if they were given a chance.
So I had to be sure and hit first."[6]

Ice hockey is a good example of a sport into which
violence generally intrudes even though it is not the
game's object to injure an opponent, as it is in boxing.
The fastest, roughest team game played, ice hockey has
been described as one whose participants are a group of
madmen with knives on their feet and clubs in their
hands, who go around beating up a piece of rubber and
one another. Tom Eccleston, who was head coach at
Providence College, has said, "I have never seen a
hockey player who played more than a year who did not
have facial scars to show." Skate blades, he once told a
conference on the medical aspects of sports, are as
sharp as razors, the sticks are lethal weapons, and the
puck, propelled from fifty to ninety miles an hour, "is a
terrific little breaker of teeth and bones." Why, then,
does someone play such a game? "Well," said Eccleston,
"you have to be partly insane; I really feel that way."[7]

Not everyone, of course, agrees that violent sports,

such as boxing and hockey, have to be banned, as has been suggested over and over by concerned groups and individuals. The answer, proponents of such sports argue, is to reform the sports. Insofar as boxing is concerned, its backers say that a closer watch should be kept on a fighter's health history; more attention should be paid to his physical fitness *before* a fight; his condition should be monitored closely *during* the fight; and blows to the head should be disqualified, or the fighters should be required to wear protective headgear.

Wrote one columnist:

> Boxing is legalized murder to the doomsayers, but to me it is a pure test of athleticism that draws upon speed, strength, stamina, intelligence and courage. The one-on-one confrontation is basic and uncomplicated. The doomsayers say it is a primitive throwback that has no place in civilized society, and perhaps it does not. But it has a place in ours. . . . Red Smith, the late columnist whose twin passions were boxing and horseracing, wrote, "They are wrong, of course, those who think boxing can be legislated out of existence. It has been tried a hundred times, but there were always men ready to fight for prizes on a barge or in a pasture lot or the back room of a saloon. It is hard to believe that a nation bereft of such men would be the stronger or better for it."[8]

It is doubtful that a total ban on boxing will ever be considered seriously, no more than would a ban on other sports that can be violent — hockey, football, and auto racing. For one thing, as Red Smith said, there will always be men who will fight for prizes somewhere. "If boxing were abolished in one state," said John M. Prenderville, chairman of the New York State Athletic Commission, after the death of Kim, "it would flourish legally in other states and countries, and illegally in the jurisdiction where it was banned. . . . A ban on boxing would be as ineffective as was Prohibition."[9]

We cannot overlook the fact, amid all this, that fighting does come naturally to many people, and it would be very difficult, if not impossible, to change such a deeply ingrained tendency. One reason for this is the close connection that exists between physical fighting — which involves the exercise of brute force to get what one wants — and what we know as competitiveness, the strong mental determination to achieve some goal. The great British philosopher Bertrand Russell has spoken of the merits of competition, saying, "I do not think that ordinary human beings can be happy without competition, for competition has been, ever since the origin of man, the spur to most serious activities." It has been said, too, that a kite rises not with the wind but against it, that our competitors are our greatest benefactors because they make us strong and sharpen our skill. Psychiatrist Chester M. Pierce of Harvard University once said of football, "It permits the demonstration of courage so as to remind and assure the great masses, in an entertaining manner, that the society has representatives able and willing to master adversity."[10]

Thus, especially for Americans who emphasize individuality and a sense of keen competition, boxing, and indeed all other sports, has an important place in molding our distinctive characters. Even tennis, after all, although it does not involve physical contact, is a duel that sharpens our reflexes and strengthens our muscles — and nurtures and allows us to express our competitive natures. Also, given what we know about aggression, sports — especially the combative ones — often enable both participant and observer to actually control violent tendencies that could erupt elsewhere with far more disastrous results. Every one of us has to let out pent-up anger sometime, to vent the steam of our frustrations. Sometimes, we do it in the wrong way. This is called *displaced aggression.* It occurs, for example, after a bad day at school or at work. A teacher gives you a hard time, is overly critical of your work; or, a boss refuses to give you a holiday, or threatens to fire you. Many people, afraid of retaliation, suppress their anger in such situations. They may want to shout at the person who has caused all the trouble, or even want to hit him or her. But they do not. So, they storm out of school or the office, fuming all the way home. And once there, they take it out on whomever they encounter first — the cat, a brother or sister, parents, or wife. Kicking the cat or yelling at a member of your family may relieve some of the suppressed rage and help you, but it's not exactly easy on your pet or the people close to you.

Sports are not the only way to let it all out. Some people kick a door, throw a book, punch a pillow, or go for a long walk. But sports are, very definitely, a way to relieve tension. Studies have demonstrated, in fact, that participating in sports does reduce internal aggression and anxiety. Moreover, athletes who engage in even the most violent sports are no more likely — indeed, they are perhaps less likely — to engage in violent behavior when not playing. It is unfortunate that a player's seeming brutality on the field, or a fighter's ferocity in the ring, often leads people to think that these men act that way all the time. The truth is that athletes can be among the mildest-mannered, most gentle of people, the stereotyped image of them as lumbering bullies notwithstanding. Even when they are playing in a rough game, they must play by strict rules, and although occasionally things get out of hand, by and large, athletes manage to keep their aggressive impulses under fairly good control considering the circumstances of the game. They are, after all, but players in a staged battle, and they, along with the officials and most of the fans, know it is just that.

But unfortunately, sometimes the fans lose sight of that fact, as well as control of themselves. It is the fan who screams "kill him" at the boxer who has an opponent reeling on the ropes, "break his arm," as a lineman charges in on a defenseless quarterback, or who shouts obscenities, hurls bottles, firecrackers, and rocks at baseball and hockey players, or who charges out onto a playing field to throw a punch at an umpire or a player, or starts a riot in the stands. One glaring example: in 1964, three hundred people were killed and five hundred injured in a riot at a soccer game in Lima, Peru.

Inflamed by the sometimes violent action before them, and quite often drunk on beer they have bought at the stadium or brought in with them, many fans behave worse than the athletes. The sports columns, too, perpetuate the violence, not by advocating it, but by their figures of speech: players are "creamed," "totaled," or "pulverized"; teams are "crushed," "demolished," and "devastated"; football scores given on radio often sound like the results of a war — "Harvard broke Brown's back 17–0," "Notre Dame stomped Army," "Alabama slaughtered Texas."

More than fifty years ago, American journalist Irvin S. Cobb described the fight fan this way: "He is a soft-fleshed, hard-faced person who keeps his own pelt safe from the bruises, but whose eyes glisten and whose hackles lift at the prospect of seeing someone else whipped to a soufflé."[11]

Dr. Stanley Cheren, an associate professor of psychiatry at Boston University School of Medicine, has studied the way sports stimulate aggressive feelings in fans. He has suggested that if the players behave badly, if they ignore the game's rules, if they fight in a sport that does not call for fighting, then the fans will often follow suit. "The fans share in much of the same emotion that grips the participants," he has said. "Witnessing struggle stimulates struggle. An event resolves or satisfies aggressive impulses in spectators only if the impulses are resolved in the conflict. Otherwise, the event stimulates aggression. It is not the amount of violence in sport that creates violence in the crowd. If that were the case, boxing matches would be very dangerous to attend. In fact, they are okay for spectators. However, let the rules get broken enough and the crowd gets ugly. The fans take sides not only in a metaphoric sense but in a real sense. They become participants."[12]

Basketball officials, Dr. Cheren adds, are well-known

for their awareness that the game's rules are a tool in managing aggression. "When they see the game getting too physical, too violent, they often call fouls more readily and re-establish control of aggressive impulses on the court. Failure to keep the aggression within the structure and rules of the game makes it contagious."[13]

While both players and officials can stop a lot of violence among fans by paying stern attention to the rules and penalizing unsportsmanlike conduct, the fans, too, bear some responsibility for keeping the games they watch relatively peaceful by making an effort to boo, rather than cheer, deliberate violence when it occurs. Dr. John Cheffers, a former football coach and professor of education at Boston University, has expressed the opinion that efforts must be made to educate or re-educate the fans. Says he, "I care about this because I'm one of those who think that sport can and should have a very constructive influence on society. I would say that the greatest value of sporting competition is that it teaches us how to handle winning and losing without becoming antisocial. When what's achieved predominates over how it's achieved, then a disrespect for the entire game, the entire sport, ensues. Violence follows disrespect. The fearful thing is that what we are now being taught to respect is violence. Sport is making it fashionable."[14]

·5·

RAPE

Rape is the sexual expression of aggression. A man committing rape doesn't do it because of desire any more than a man who drinks does it because he's thirsty.

— DR. NICHOLAS GROTH, *director of the sex offender program at the Connecticut Correctional Institution*

RAPE. THE VERY WORD SHOUTS VIOLENCE. It is, in truth, as *Time* magazine's theater critic, T. E. Kalem, has put it, "a four-letter word that screams."[1] Kalem used the phrase in a review of a play about rape, *Extremities,* in which the intended victim turns on her attacker.

As a literary theme, rape appears quite often. Shakespeare wrote of it in *Titus Andronicus,* and in *The Rape of Lucrece.* It was the subject of the Japanese film *Rashomon,* and an American movie, *Straw Dogs.* In art, too, rape has been depicted — notably in the celebrated *Rape of the Sabines,* a marble group by the Italian sculptor Gionnani da Bologna showing the abduction of a Sabine maiden by a Roman; and in a painting by Lucca Giordano showing Romulus, the legendary founder of Rome, directing the Romans as they seize resisting women.

But rape, in real life, goes far beyond where any artful portrayal can go. It is our most rapidly increasing crime. In 1948, some eight thousand cases of rape were reported, most of them so-called statutory rape. Statutory rape means sexual relations with a female under the legal age of consent, usually eighteen, even if she agrees. The other legal classification of rape is forcible rape. And it is forcible rape that has steadily increased. In 1962, according to the FBI, there were about sixteen thousand cases; in 1971, some forty-two thousand; today, the figure is around eighty thousand. Moreover, a few years ago the U.S. Justice Department disclosed that in cities surveyed, a third of all rapes were gang rapes — that is, they were committed by two or more offenders. One such case gained national notoriety early in 1983. It involved six men charged with raping a twenty-one-year-old woman for two hours in a tavern in New Bedford, Massachusetts, while patrons of the bar cheered them on. Thousands of people marched in protest of the attack carrying placards that read, "Rape is Hate," "Rape is Violence," and "Rape is Not a Spectator Sport."[2]

The vicious attack, and others like it, proves that gang rape is not always associated only with war and assaults on villages and cities by conquering soldiers who regard women as spoils of battle. It has become a serious problem in most of our cities and towns, and chances are that the communities that have not reported a rape have remained silent because officials and families want to spare the victim embarrassment and further emotional trauma.

Rape — along with murder, incest, adultery, abortion, and all sorts of other sex-related activities — has been a blot on society's record for millions of years. Writes anthropologist Helen E. Fisher of the New School for Social Research in New York City, "Rape is common in many species, including our close cousins the orangutans, and it is committed in all human cultures. It is particularly prevalent among the Eskimos and South American Indians. In fact, among some Brazilian tribes, gang rape is a legitimate means of punishing promiscuous women."[3]

Contrary to what many people think, rape is not merely forceful gratification of a sexual desire. It is, rather, a violent crime, an aggressive sexual act by an emotionally sick person. As sex researcher Virginia Johnson has explained it, "Rape is not to be confused with love-making. It is not primarily sexual or erotic, but rather an expression of hostility, of power, of exercising control over a helpless victim." Dr. Groth, whose remark precedes this chapter, underscores the point that force is what rape is all about. Sex offenders he has worked with, in fact, were sexually active people at the time of their crimes, he says, and were not driven by frustration or pent-up sexual urges.[4]

Rape, it is obvious, causes both emotional and physical harm to the victim. Victims commonly have what psychiatrists call rape trauma syndrome. This was described recently in the *Journal of the American Medical*

Association by a group from the University of Kentucky College of Medicine and the Lexington (Kentucky) Rape Crisis Center. Immediately after a woman is raped, the physicians explained, some women may display a wide range of emotions openly, while others hide their feelings and appear quite composed.[5]

Among the feelings a rape victim usually reports are shock, disbelief, anxiety, humiliation, shame, guilt, and self-blame. Fear of death and injury are, of course, especially strong and can recur if the rape happened in a supposedly safe place, such as at home or work. "That woman in New Bedford is never going to be comfortable in a group of men again because she will always be suspicious," a member of the staff of a Boston rape crisis center predicted recently. "She will never know."[6] A woman who has been raped may, hours or months later, also feel physically tired, have tension headaches, startle easily, and be unable to sleep, especially if she was awakened from sleep by the assault. She may lose her appetite, or she may become nauseated when she thinks of the assault.

Recovery from rape can be very slow, the doctors who investigated rape trauma syndrome said. The victim may suffer depression and nightmares and changes in her menstrual habits; she may become suddenly fearful if she sees a man who resembles her attacker; she may find it difficult to go out alone; she may move or change her telephone number frequently; and in a common complication, she may develop a dislike for sexual activity, or find less pleasure in such intimacy. A report on victims of rape points out:

It has indeed been suggested that forcible rape be removed from the penal code and that the rapist be tried, if necessary and applicable, for assault. This suggestion, however, made in order to liberate the woman from sex-specific laws and humiliating treatment by law enforcers, does not adequately deal with the problem. The social meaning of rape is very different from assault. While both assault and rape are basically acts of aggression, and hostility, sexual assault or rape is a total attack against the whole person, affecting the victim's physical, psychological and social identity. Hardly any other crime can be committed against a woman with a comparable traumatic impact. Assault, on the other hand, is a much more impersonal and less intimate attack on a person; rape, moreover, does not necessarily include serious elements of violence and assault, but may happen simply because the victim is intimidated. She may fear that resistance would be futile, dangerous, or she may even be paralyzed by fear and unable to do anything at all.[7]

Although rape is most often directed against women, men, too, are raped. Adult males are frequently raped in prison by homosexuals, young boys are raped by men who sometimes murder them afterward. Men are also occasionally raped by women. Those who have been so assaulted experience some of the same problems women do, including loss of self-esteem and impaired sexual functioning.

But whether a man rapes a woman or a woman rapes a man, the sexual "high" that may result, as some psychiatrists believe, comes not from sexual self-satisfaction but from terrifying the victim. Most rapists, psychologists and policemen know, are hostile people, often with criminal records for aggressive assaults. Here is how a typical rapist has been described by one specialist in human behavior:

> This antisocial psychopath is a cold, seemingly unfeeling man who has always taken what he has wanted from others without apparent concern for the feelings of his victims or for the consequences of his act. For him, rape is just another instance of aggressive taking, except that in this case he steals sexual satisfaction rather than money or property. When questioned about his offense, he often responds with callous sarcasm, completely devoid of guilt or concern. He may well simply respond with the statement, "I wanted it so I took it." The rape fits so well with his character structure and is so typical of his general behavior pattern that he can see nothing wrong with the act, and often goes on to rationalize that the victim probably enjoyed it. He wants no part of therapy unless he sees it as a means of manipulating his way out of incarceration. Needless to say, he is just as difficult to treat as those psychopaths who commit non-sexual offenses.[8]

Rape can be impulsive or it can be planned. It can be done by one man, or, as we have noted, by several. It may be accompanied by more violence — beating, choking, wounding with a knife — as the rapist tries to get the woman to submit; or, the rapist may simply threaten physical harm if the woman does not comply. The rapist does not always skulk about in alleys, or leap out at his victims from behind trees and bushes, or break into his victims' homes. As the prosecutor of a recent rape case in New York put it recently, "Some of them wear three-piece suits and rent limousines and take their victims to shows and dinner before luring them back to their apartments."[9]

Many times, a rape victim is murdered to prevent her from identifying her assailant. The following case, involving a teenager who committed twelve rapes over a four-year period and murdered five of his victims, is a summary of one that appeared in a recent issue of the *American Journal of Psychiatry* and is a chilling example of the seriousness of the crime and the nature of the rapist:[10]

The young rapist involved was of average intelligence, but was withdrawn from high school in his senior year because of excessive absenteeism and lack of progress. He was outgoing, athletically inclined, and had a close circle of friends, male and female. He saw himself as a leader rather than a follower. When he was nine years old, he and some other boys were caught writing four-letter words on the sidewalk by the school principal. When he was twelve, he broke into an apartment and stole property valued at one hundred dollars; at thirteen, he was charged with driving without a license; at fourteen, with burglary and rape, petty larceny and stealing a car. He admitted using alcohol and drugs, worked occasionally during his high school years, and was subsequently sent to a psychiatric institution. He was discharged after eighteen months on the recommendation that he live at home and continue psychotherapy on a weekly outpatient basis. Three weeks after he returned home, he was charged with attempted armed robbery, and some time later with the murders.

His victims ranged in age from seventeen to thirty-four; he knew three by sight, but the other nine were total strangers. Most of his victims were approached at knife point as they entered the elevator in their apartment buildings. Here is how this troubled young man described his thinking before his third murder: "I was thinking, I've killed two. I might as well kill this one, too. Something in me was wanting to kill. I tied her up with her stockings and started to walk away. Then I heard her through the woods kind of rolling around and making muffled sounds. And I turned back and said, 'No, I have to kill her. I've got to do this to preserve and protect myself.' " One of his rape victims was luckier. "She told me her father was dying of cancer," the young man said. "I thought of my own brother who had cancer. I couldn't kill her. She had it bad already." Because his aggression was apparently cooled by his identifying with her situation, he ran off.

One must wonder, of course, what made this young man commit such terrible crimes. It is known that as he grew angrier with some of his victims — one scratched his face, for example, and started to run — his aggressive behavior worsened, and he killed to show his authority; he also killed when he became fearful his victims might talk. But there is more to it than that. The authors of the journal report, among them Robert K. Ressler of the FBI Academy's Behavioral Science Unit, had this to say about the youthful murderer's motives: "The modern view of rape regards it as an act of violence expressing power as one motive. We suggest that the psychological motive of power expands for the rapist-murderer from a need for power over one person to a need for power over a collective group." By that, the authors meant that while the rapist-murderer was pleased that some of his victims were not reporting or identifying him — indicative of his feeling of power over them individually — he was also happy over his ability to fool, for a time, police, psychiatrists, and judges. That ability to fool the authorities is what makes a rapist so dangerous. Not only is it probable that he has committed the crime more times, say, than the one he may be charged with, but there is also still a tendency for many law-enforcement officials to believe a rapist when he claims that the woman brought it on herself by dressing provocatively, or by leading him on verbally, or that the woman was only retaliating with a rape charge because she had been jilted by the man. If such things happen, they are exceedingly rare, as is false identification of a rapist by the victim. Still, it is a sad commentary that it is usually the number of physical injuries a woman suffers at the hands of a rapist, the degree of violence, that influences the judgment of relatives, friends, hospital personnel, and the police. Simply put, if the victim has a lot of physical injuries and she was attacked by a stranger, her story is believed; if there are no bruises, and her attacker is known to her, chances are she will not be believed. "[People] tend to express more doubt and give less support to victims who have no visible injuries or who were raped by someone they knew," said the physicians who wrote the *Journal of the American Medical Association* article mentioned earlier. "Despite the recent shift away from thinking of rape as a sexual experience to realizing that it is a violent assault, there is still a tendency to see the victim as responsible, thereby increasing her guilt."[11]

When rapists are convicted they usually draw long prison sentences because of the danger that they will repeat the crime. Sometimes, the penalty for rape is death. There have been suggestions that rapists be treated with calming drugs, or by castration, the surgical removal of their testicles to suppress their sex drive. Others argue that more effort should be made to rehabilitate the rapist.

There is no question that such people need help, but the victim of a rapist needs much more. She suffers incredibly, as we have seen, and sometimes for a very long time after the incident. Not only does she require proper medical treatment for her physical injuries, but she also needs sensitive listeners, family and friends, who will encourage her to talk of the experience. If she is unwilling to talk to those close to her, then she should be encouraged to talk to a professional counselor, a clergyman, or to the staff of a rape crisis center. Least of all should she be ignored, especially if she seems to have composed herself and forgotten the incident.

Rapists strike women of all ages, from infants to the very elderly, and all of us, no matter our age or sex, should be alert to that side of violence, and to help whenever we can.

·6·

DOMESTIC VIOLENCE

*A life is beautiful and ideal or the reverse,
only when we have taken into our consideration the social as well as the family relationship.*

—— HAVELOCK ELLIS

IT IS HARD TO IMAGINE, unless we have had firsthand experience, a family in which children are brutally beaten
or killed by parents, in which wives are assaulted by
husbands, and parents beaten by children. The family,
after all, is supposed to be the centerpiece of our society, a supporting, loving unit that reflects nothing but
harmony.

But this image is not always true. Families do have
problems. Teenagers rebel and run away from home, or
get into trouble with the law or with drugs and alcohol.
Husbands leave wives, wives leave husbands, and family
arguments, some of them heated, are common. We
grudgingly have come to accept such events as part of
living together in a group; they are the expected reactions to the tensions that come with such an arrange-
ment.

But family squabbles are minor compared to the incidents of family violence that have become increasingly evident over the past few years. It has been estimated that nearly two million women are beaten by their husbands every year, that two million children are victims of abuse, and that some two thousand children die each year of the beatings they receive at the hands of parents. "Social norms approve of one family member's right to hit another when there is wrong-doing and when that person will not listen to reason," writes Dr. Jeanne F. Arnold, of the Department of Community and Family Medicine at Dartmouth Medical School. "Opinion surveys have found that one sixth to one fourth of both men and women feel that there is justification for one partner's hitting a spouse at some time. . . . Media attention is given the wife who shoots her husband or the woman who is beaten into a coma by her angry mate. Society then rationalizes that victims come from lower-income families who have different cultural values and that, further, the wife probably 'deserved what she got' and perhaps really enjoys such treatment as a sign of affection. . . . Child abuse and intramarital physical attacks take place in families of all races, ages, economic classes, educational backgrounds and religions; in rural and suburban families, in families that are intact and in those that have been sundered by divorce or separation. . . . Domestic violence accounts for 60 percent of all police calls, and one quarter of all homicides are the result of some kind of family dispute."[1]

Given the current level of violence, it should come as no surprise that domestic violence is so widespread. Thus, we cannot consider such violence as a separate problem; it is, really, just another spin-off of society's difficulties, and the reactions of individuals to certain stresses and to particular characteristics of their makeup, whether genetic, psychological, or social. A wife beater could be the same sociopath who goes around breaking windows for the fun of it, or who gets into fights at the least provocation. The child abuser is probably no different. Both kinds of men, and women who abuse children, may well have been abused themselves as children, or watched their fathers assault their wives. Poverty, and unemployment, too, may have something to do with it, as they do in all other kinds of violence. There are numerous examples of this. Recently, in Brooklyn, New York, a man stabbed his wife to death because, he said, he lost his temper over her constant complaints about his inability to hold down a job. The newspaper account of the incident went on to say that at the Victim Services Agency, about a quarter of the battered women who call crisis hot lines say that the men abusing them have recently lost their jobs. It quoted an economist at New York University's Urban Research Center as saying, "Unemployment destabilizes the traditional family structures, neighborhoods and communities. The link isn't direct, but unemployment leads to alcoholism and many types of family stress, and those factors lead to violence." Said a psychologist of some of the inmates at the jail on Riker's Island, "They're so frustrated, so they strike out first at their families. Because the men can't get jobs, they have accepted the reverse role in the family and are staying home with the children while the wife works.

They just weren't prepared for the frustrations of child-rearing and they end up abusing their children."[2]

Unemployment is not the only reason for family violence. To begin with, the role that cultural tradition plays in bringing violence about and in preventing it cannot be ignored. There are, thus, certain "rules" that govern violent behavior within a particular group. For example, hitting or verbal abuse is tolerated in many Italian families if the aggressive behavior is directed against a family member who has brought disgrace or embarrassment on the family. Murder of kin to uphold a family's honor occurs frequently among Arab Muslims. We also know that many cultures, including that of the Chinese, had a long history of using infanticide — the killing of a child — to get rid of unwanted daughters. In ancient Sparta, defective children were hurled to their deaths from the top of Mount Taygetus, and in Africa, in the South Pacific, and among our own American Indians, it was not uncommon for the younger members of a family to do away with the elderly members when they became decrepit and lost their capacity to work.

But the domestic violence that troubles us today is a good deal different from those examples from the past. It also goes far beyond any cultural tradition, for in America it occurs among virtually all the ethnic groups that make up our nation. Thus, it is a social problem. It often occurs in families simply because society still regards violence as a legitimate way to react, to keep things in hand, to discipline, to get revenge.

Consider child abuse. It stands as a glaring example of how some adults attempt to control, take revenge on a family member who has broken a "rule," or take out personal frustrations and insecurity. Rarely, if ever, is the victim at fault in cases of true child abuse. We are not talking here about the light tap on the cheek or the rear end of a child who has irritated his or her mother or dad. Although some child psychologists argue that all forms of physical aggression, no matter how minor, are to be condemned, this is not the sort of child abuse that has medical specialists and police departments alarmed. There are many examples, most of them horrifying to read and hear about. Consider the following case, which occurred in 1983 in New York City. A young father became angry with his three-year-old son for reasons that were unclear. He punched the boy, then beat him across the back with a leather strap. He then dragged the boy off, tied him up, and hung him upside down on a clothesline from a third floor window, and left him there for more than ten minutes. If it had not been for a neighbor who heard the boy crying and cut him down, the child might have died. The father, who reportedly had threatened to throw the child off the roof, was charged with attempted murder and assault.[3] Bad as this case is, there have been much worse, many of them involving sexual abuse, and many ending in the mutilation or death of the child.

Usually, one hears of the cases in which very young children are abused; because a young child is especially vulnerable, these are the incidents that generally receive widespread media attention. But according to specialists in adolescent medicine, adolescents, too, are abused. "They are likely to be on the receiving end of abuse in different ways than they were as children," says one report on the subject. "Sexual molestation may become physically violent as the abusing family member becomes jealous of relationships the adolescent forms outside the family. Mothers are the primary abusers of young children until adolescence when fathers are more likely to punish because an adolescent's 'undesirable' behavior is seen as more critical. Punishment thus may have more severe physical consequences for the adolescent."[4] The report also quoted one specialist as saying, moreover, that adolescents who are abused are more likely than others to find violence acceptable, to leave home early and not complete their education, and to become violent partners in their own marriages.

The point about the young who were abused becoming abusers themselves is a telling one, and one that keeps appearing in reports of mistreated children. It is not difficult to understand. When a young man and woman become parents, they have not, really, trained for the job. In fact, they received infinitely more training when they learned how to drive an automobile and got their licenses. People learn how to be parents pretty much "on the job." They feel their way through it, making mistakes, learning from them, and in most cases, doing pretty well in the end. But about all they can draw on is what they have learned in their own homes, from their parents. And too often, parents know no other way of "teaching" a child than by using physical punishment. Their dictum, "Spare the rod and spoil the child," may start out with good intentions; but often, that philosophy gets out of hand, and they spank to an extreme. Children who have been treated harshly cannot help being affected by the hostile actions of their parents, and when they grow up and have their own children, they find it difficult to be tolerant; so they respond by being aggressive. Studies by Dr. Shervert Frazier, a psychiatrist at Harvard Medical School, found some years ago that repeated brutalization as a small child by parents or parent substitutes turned up in the backgrounds of some people who later killed a relative or family member. Dr. Frazier also found out several other things. One was that the murderers experienced long periods of loneliness during childhood. Another was that they lacked the ability to play games. Moreover, the murderers had low feelings of their worth and experienced a good deal of humiliation as children.

Other factors besides being abused as a child play a part, too. One is poor marital adjustment. According to social-work specialists at the University of Texas at Austin, child abusers tend to be young parents with marital problems who are psychologically immature. Alcohol or drug abuse is another consideration and is, according to the Texas group, involved in approximately 50 percent of child-abuse cases. Said Dr. Clayton T. Shorkey, associate professor of social work, "Alcohol or drug abuse may essentially increase the parents' inability to deal with a whole range of stresses in their situation." Dr. Shorkey also observed that parents who abuse their children also tend to have very low self-esteem. Associated with that is the feeling among abusing parents that they have no sense of control over their lives, that external forces are controlling what goes on. So, to try to gain control some parents use violence, often directing it at a particular child. Sadly, the child at whom the violence is aimed is often mentally retarded, or someone with other physical or learning disabilities. Sometimes, this sort of abuse may be tied to unrealistic expectations parents have of their children. "They have certain ideas as to what is appropriate or inappropriate behavior for a particular child at a particular age," said one specialist, "and as a result they make certain demands on that child to perform accordingly." Moreover, some abusing parents are unable to tell the difference between bad behavior and a bad person. Thus, rather than try to change bad behavior these parents assume that the child is a bad person who needs to be punished or condemned.[5]

Other experts have suggested that raising twins places enough stress on parents to increase the risk of child abuse in these families. Other studies indicate that child-abuse rates are higher in large families and in families where there are short time periods between births. The increased stress of child-rearing under such conditions has been blamed for the higher rate. In a recent report in the journal *Pediatrics,* doctors who conducted a study of child abuse concluded that although such abuse results from a complex mix of many factors, parents should be aware of the enormous physical and economic demands they will have with two infants. Furthermore, they found that in families with twins, siblings were victims more frequently than the twins themselves — a finding that suggests that the birth of twins places tremendous stress on the entire family.[6]

But serious as the stress is on the family as a whole, it is obvious that the child who is abused suffers the most. Apart from the physical scars, which can be unbelievably disfiguring, there are the invisible ones left on the young minds. There is the guilt that a child often feels for having done something wrong to deserve such punishment. There is hatred for the parent who strikes the child. Young girls are likely to leave home and perhaps turn to prostitution. Boys may turn into bullies. Worse, there is the possibility of suicide. According to Dr. Eva Deykin, a Harvard School of Public Health epidemiologist, many teens who attempt suicide come from families with a history of violence. "There are theoretical reasons why such associations may exist," says Dr. Deykin. "First, violence is a learned response to frustration and anger. An individual who has been exposed to child abuse might incorporate that response, turning aggression inward, as a means of coping with outside infringements."[7] Second, children who have been abused have very low self-esteem, a characteristic that has been identified with suicide attempts.

It should be noted here that not all the violence directed at children is physical. Verbal abuse, rejection, or neglect can be just as devastating to a child as a blow. One might also ask whether spanking is a form of child abuse. Dr. Eli Newberger, director of the Family Development Clinic at the Children's Hospital Medical Center in Boston, answers the question this way: "The role of corporal punishment in child rearing is still controversial. In fact, only four states have outlawed it in the schools. Although some child development specialists say that physical force is acceptable in certain circumstances, most agree that it should never be used on children under two years of age. My own personal feeling is that parents should never resort to physical force. There are positive, loving ways to teach acceptable behavior. Sparing the rod does not mean spoiling the child. We as a society can help prevent child abuse by rejecting violence as a method for resolving human conflict. We have everything to gain by rearing the next generation in peace."[8]

For those who may regard such wise words as somewhat unrealistic, consider for a moment a tribe of Indians, the Tarahumara, in Mexico's Sierra Madres. Violence among the Tarahumaras is virtually unknown. There are no police, no soldiers, no jails, no crime. Over the last fifty years, there has been no stealing, even though the Indians are poor, and only two murders have been reported among the fifty thousand tribal members. Nor have there been any suicides — in fact, the Tarahumara language does not have a word for suicide.

Why do these Indians behave in such a model way?

The answer comes from Dr. Louis J. West, chairman of the Department of Psychiatry and Behavioral Science at UCLA School of Medicine, who has spent a lot of time studying the tribe and its customs. "It all comes down to how the children are reared," says Dr. West. "The Tarahumara Indians never physically punish their children for anything. To inflict pain upon a child, or to threaten to do so is beyond the tribe's comprehension. If a child does anything wrong, and it does happen, others will just stare at him, perhaps even laugh, and the child will finally hang his head in shame. You just know that the youngster will never commit that wrong again. Shame is a much more powerful extinguisher of undesired behavior in children than punishment."[9]

As long as American children grow up in an atmosphere full of violence, there seems to be little likelihood that child abuse will be abolished. About the only thing that can be done under the present circumstances is to try to identify the situations that make it likely to occur. According to Dr. Newberger, because family problems that are associated with child abuse may be evident very early, help and support must be offered to parents and caretakers of young children. Dr. Newberger points out that many abused children are handicapped or have special needs. "That's one reason," he says, "why early identification of special needs is so important. We see many patients at our hospital whose conditions have caused family crisis and upheaval because a diagnosis was made so late. A child with a hearing disorder, for example, might be regarded as disobedient; a child with a learning disorder as uncooperative; a child with a seizure disorder as unresponsive and listless. Many of these problems, as well as the more obvious physical handicaps, provoke abusive behavior from parents under stress." Families are often relieved when these problems are identified, says Dr. Newberger. "The child can begin to receive appropriate therapy and treatment, and the family unit can be strengthened, when necessary, through counseling."[10]

Apprehension and punishment of the child abuser is another way to lessen the problem. All states now have legislation that requires that child-abuse incidents be reported, and many have criminal penalties for failure to report. Since an abusing parent is the least likely one to report such a case, the burden lies with other members of the family, neighbors, teachers, and with physicians, who often see the abused children in hospital emergency rooms. Thus, again, it is up to us to be alert for evidence of child abuse, and to at least make known our concern when it is suspected. Obviously, we have no right to accuse someone on the basis of flimsy evidence; there is always the danger of false accusation in cases when violence, or any crime, is committed. But there is nothing wrong with confiding our suspicions to a close friend, to a clergyman or teacher, or even to a policeman. It is better to tell someone about the possibility of an act of violence occurring than to read about it later in the newspapers and regret that you did not speak up sooner. Often we read interviews with neighbors who, after a member of the community has been arrested for child abuse or murder, declare, "Well, we always had a feeling that would happen." Or, "Well, we're not surprised." If these people had expressed some apprehension earlier, the violent act might have been prevented.

In general, though, people have become more aware of the problem of child abuse, and it has received much media attention lately. For many reasons, however, the same awareness does not always apply to spouse abuse. True, articles discussing the battered wife and the prevalence of the problem appear regularly in newspapers and magazines. But the actual incidents of wife abuse — which is more widespread than husband abuse — are not reported as frequently as the cases involving a battered child. It is usually only when a wife has been murdered by a husband that the issue is aired fully.

Sometimes, women themselves are too afraid to report that they have been beaten; they fear the husband might retaliate and beat them more. They may also be ashamed to discuss such incidents with others. Or, they may feel they were at fault for provoking a husband to assault them, and so they remain silent. When police are called, they often find it difficult to determine — unless the woman shows serious injuries — whether a family spat or a beating has occurred. Thus, police sometimes dismiss such incidents, and write them down in their reports as merely a "domestic argument." Friends and neighbors may also be of little help. Sometimes, they are reluctant to get involved in personal family trouble; at other times, they may encourage the woman, who may have left home after an incident, to return to a husband and "try to work it out." Such advice only confirms any feelings a woman may have that it was she who was at fault. Some people also believe that women are masochistic — that is, that they enjoy being beaten. Others say that they are free to leave whenever they want, but that they do not because abusive husbands often promise never to do it again, beg for forgiveness, or excuse their behavior simply by saying they just lost their heads temporarily.

What kind of man beats his wife? Again, as was said in the discussion of the causes of violence and assassins, it is difficult to arrive at any definite answer. A recent report in the *American Journal of Psychiatry* cites the common characteristics of violent husbands as described by Margaret Elbow, director of the Family Service Association in Lubbock, Texas.[11] They are as follows:

- The controller. This man has an emotional need to control others, is used to getting his own way, and is never to blame. People are important to him only if they can do something for him; he rarely does anything for others. Violence erupts when the controller feels he is no longer in charge, as when his authority is questioned. His basic fear is that he will lose control. It is theorized that perhaps his wife symbolizes a parent who controlled him, and allowed him little room for autonomy as a child.

- The defender. This man needs to protect himself, to strike before he is struck. He is not afraid of being controlled, but of being harmed. He needs a woman who will cling to him and depend on him so he can feel strong. The defender's wife stands for a parent who assumed he was aggressive and driven by evil forces. He anticipates she will also punish and overpower him for being assertive or sexual. Therefore, he has to keep her powerless so he will not be vulnerable. His opposition to his wife's leaving him stems from his need to have a defenseless person to protect.

- The approval seeker. This man must be continually praised. When he abuses his wife, each incident is related to his feelings about himself. When his self-esteem is down he expects rejection and behaves in such a way as to precipitate it.

- The incorporator. This man needs to incorporate the strengths of another to experience himself as a whole.

He is desperate in that he needs to cling to his mate, and the more she withdraws, the greater is his need to incorporate. If his wife threatens to leave, this often makes matters worse.

Many of these traits, of course, appear in men who do not beat their wives. Thus, it is not always easy to accurately identify the man who will behave badly at home. Many wife beaters are Dr. Jekyll and Mr. Hyde characters — that is, they are mean and violent at one moment, and charming, kind, and contrite at another. If you meet such a person when he is in a good mood, it is highly unlikely you would ever suspect him, unless you knew his history.

Abuse also takes many forms. The type we usually hear about involves an actual beating. And sometimes, even that is often seen as part of family hassles, and is even accepted. But there are other forms of abuse. A husband may regularly insult his wife, or bruise her self-esteem by telling her she is too fat, a lousy cook and housekeeper; he might tell her he is sorry he ever married her, that he drinks heavily just to get away from her nagging. Behavior like that can be as devastating as a blow with a fist or a slap, but it is not the sort of abuse that a woman can rely on in court if she is trying to prove her husband is abusing her.

In the final analysis, wife abuse is closely associated with power and who has it in the family. Men have long believed that they are in charge, that their word is final in everything from financial matters to disciplining the children. When such long-held beliefs are thwarted —

by a wife who asserts herself, who stands up for her rights to be treated as an equal partner — a man may lose control and demonstrate his power by striking out with a violent act. And understandably, sometimes the violent behavior of the husband brings a violent reaction from the wife. It is not known just how many women kill their husbands every year in response to abuse, but it happens. (One estimate puts the number at two thousand cases a year.)[12]

Such a violent reaction may seem justified to people familiar with the details of a certain case. But it is not always easy to convince a court. Moreover, many authorities still question whether enough scientific knowledge about what is called the battered woman syndrome exists to permit psychologists and psychiatrists to testify as expert witnesses on the subject. When, for example, a New Jersey woman was tried for killing her husband with a pair of scissors in 1980, after seven years of battering and abuse, the court would not admit expert psychological testimony. The woman was convicted of reckless manslaughter and sentenced to five years in prison. Her case, at this writing, is pending before the New Jersey Supreme Court. According to the American Psychological Association, which filed a friend of the court brief in the case, psychologists would have expressed the opinion that because the defendant suffered from the battered woman syndrome, she reasonably believed it was necessary to use deadly force in the struggle with her husband in order to prevent death or great bodily harm to herself and her children. "As to the question of whether adequate scientific knowledge of the battered woman syndrome actually exists," says the APA, "court opinions in other jurisdictions, the scientific literature, the law review commentary and the number of researchers and scientific materials in the field of battered woman syndrome all indicate that methodology employed by these researchers is generally accepted by the relevant scientific community and that the field is well developed with a sound psychological basis." APA concluded that enough is known to permit qualified experts to form a reliable opinion as to whether a defendant was suffering from the syndrome and whether, as a result, she reasonably believed it was necessary to act in self-defense.[13]

As future fathers and mothers, each of you has the potential to be an abusive parent. As future husbands and wives, each of you will at one time or another become verbally abusive; some of you may use your hands rather than your mouths. Because men are far more likely to assault or kill, you must, if you are a young man, change the way you feel about women if the way you feel is based on machismo, on putting women in their places, on a regard for women as mere objects for sex, housework, and nonthinking pursuits. It is men with such attitudes who are at the gravest risk of becoming abusers. Learn how to express your feelings without using your fists, how to communicate with words, and learn to ask yourself, every time you are irritated at a young woman who asserts herself, why is it all right for you to do so, but not for her?

At a recent meeting of the American Orthopsychiatric Association, David Adams, a therapist at a Boston counseling service, gave an eloquent talk on men and violence. In it, he made the following apt remarks:

> While many sexist attitudes and expectations on the part of men are sometimes conscious, others are individually or collectively unconscious. For instance, men unwittingly expect women to be their emotional caretakers, ego massagers, and guardians of the relationship. In fact, we commonly hold women responsible for our discontent, so much so that when we are unhappy (for whatever reason) we often blame our partners or mothers because they are more available and accountable than our jobs, our bosses, the economy, or our feelings about ourselves. The trouble with these kinds of expectations is that men typically hate feeling dependent — and we often go to great lengths to show that we are independent, self-sufficient, and fully in control of our lives. Not only do we deny our dependency on women, but we devalue the human qualities and caretaking skills that are identified with women. . . . The devaluation of women also serves as a necessary precondition to violence toward women. Once you have devalued someone, or a particular class of people, you make it more acceptable to abuse and exploit them. . . .
>
> Male identity, as we presently know it, is socially constructed and learned. As it is socially constructed, it means having superiority and control over women. In practice, it means relating to women as possessions rather than as people or partners. Tragically, at present there is no more common way for a boy or man to confirm his male identity in our culture than by denigrating or exploiting women. Boys learn from an early age that being a boy means being better than girls and this basic

attitude, with minor refinements, is carried into male adulthood. There is nothing inherently masculine about these attitudes toward women. We can change the ways that masculinity is defined and understood. Men must take an active part in recasting the mold.[14]

·7·

PRISON

The vilest deeds like poison weeds
Bloom well in prison air:
It is only what is good in man
That wastes and withers there:
Pale Anguish keeps the heavy gate
And the Warder is Despair.

— OSCAR WILDE

THOSE OMINOUS WORDS FROM THE *Ballad of Reading Gaol* were written in 1898, but they are as accurate today as they were then. Indeed, consider these more contemporary observations by Frank Schmalleger, associate professor of criminal justice at Pembroke State University in North Carolina: "It has been said that prison is a sort of graduate school of crime. In American prisons, inmates learn more than new criminal techniques. They acquire, through association with diverse criminal types, additional socialization into criminal reality. It is in prison that careerists from different criminal subcultures come into close contact, and it is in prison that the wellsprings of a national criminal culture are nourished. Drug dealers, robbers, con men, pimps, who might never meet on the outside, can communicate face-to-face in prison. The result is a bond of common interest and attitude. The occasional criminal who says he is sorry, who expresses guilt and shame and admits, 'I didn't mean to do it,' is despised and ridiculed by inmate society."[1]

There are nearly four hundred thousand inmates in state and federal prisons in the United States, and the number is increasing. More than eight hundred are on death row, waiting to be executed, or waiting for appeals to be heard by the courts. The cost of supporting this vast system is about five billion dollars a year, much more than is spent to run many of our states. To care for and guard just one inmate for one year, in fact, comes to around fifteen to twenty thousand dollars — about twice as much as it costs for one year of college.

But despite the enormous expenditure, there is no sign that the money has done much to lessen the nation's troubles with crime and violence. Moreover, our prisons are overcrowded, generally ineffective, and violent. Some years ago, Elvis Presley could sing jovially about "dancin' to the jailhouse rock." But such antics are, it should go without saying, true only in song. "In no institution is human ecology more seriously breached and eroded than in prisons," says a study by Project Fisherman, a Massachusetts program that helps public offenders cope with life on the outside. "The physical and social conditions of boredom, loneliness, homosexuality, and distrust breed attitudes of resentment and revenge. The 66 percent rate of recidivism [repeat offenses] in Massachusetts, not unlike other states, speaks for itself."[2]

It is no wonder that the U.S. prison system has been likened to a time bomb ticking its way to an explosion. Riots have become common and prisoners bolder. At the state prison in Ossining, New York (formerly known as Sing Sing prison), in January of 1983, inmates held seventeen guards hostage for two days, freeing them only after inmate demands were read over television. The incident was nowhere near as serious as the Attica uprising mentioned previously, but it is another bit of evidence that tempers in prison run high.

While prison may remove some of the most violent offenders from public view, it does not, however, put an end to violence. The goal of law-enforcement officials is often to punish rather than help a criminal — an approach we will look at in a bit more depth in the following chapter — and, as is true in most prisons, punishment has merely taken some of the violence off the streets and shifted it indoors. Prison gangs operate freely behind bars, extorting money from fellow inmates, dealing in drugs, and murdering prisoners. In California, prison gangs — with names like Nuestra Familia (Our Family), the Mexican Mafia, the Aryan Brotherhood, and the Black Guerrilla Family — have murdered more than one hundred persons and injured many others in prisons over the past eight years. In Illinois, 75 percent of the fourteen thousand prisoners belong to prison gangs. And in Walla Walla, Washington, recently, two convict groups smuggled deadly cyanide poison into the state prison, but the prison staff seized it before it was used. "It was pretty clear their purpose was to put cyanide in the food to kill both staff and inmates," said Walter Kautzky, the state's director of prisons. "They wanted to create chaos and anarchy."[3]

In such a place where, as the writer Oscar Wilde said, the vilest deeds bloom well, it is only the rare man or woman (women account for 4 percent of the prison population, but their number has increased 25 percent in the last few years) who comes away from prison with higher motives than when he or she went in. As Jack Schaller of the American Institute of Criminal Justice in Pennsylvania has observed, "Prisons only serve to embitter those inside them. You remove [people] from society, put them in a time capsule with a lot of hardened criminals in terrible conditions, throw them back on the street five years later, and expect them to be better citizens. In most cases, they're much worse."[4]

More than likely, that means that the ex-convict will commit a crime again, and wind up back in jail. Chances are he or she will return to the old neighborhood where the same poverty, the same easy attitude toward crime, will prevail. The ex-convict runs out of release money fast, finding a decent job is difficult if not impossible, banks often refuse to open a checking account or give credit. It is easy to see why, faced with so dim a future, many men and women return to their old ways. Sometimes, too, they do it deliberately almost as soon as they get out because they know it is not easy to make it on the outside; and, they know that getting caught will mean free food, clothing, and a place to sleep in a prison that is bad, but often not nearly so bad or uncertain as life on the outside.

For many years, criminologists and concerned citizens have agonized over the prison system, and have offered many suggestions to improve it. But there have been very few noteworthy changes. One difficulty is that no one seems to agree on whether prisons should exist to punish or restrain a criminal, or whether they should be places where a criminal is rehabilitated — changed for the better. The answer may well be: both. Former U.S. Attorney General William French Smith put it quite bluntly in a recent speech, saying, "Murderers, rapists, and other violent criminals, drug traffickers and habitual offenders belong in prisons, and they must stay in prisons. Prisons are necessary for those who pose serious threats to society or for whom anything less than a prison sentence would unduly minimize the seriousness of their offense."[5]

These remarks are well founded. There are, after all, degrees of crime, and differences in the makeup of each criminal. A violent offender is generally quite different from the white-collar crook who pays his dues in one of the so-called country clubs — low-security prisons where the inmates live comfortably without the brutalization and humiliation that are the hallmarks of the maximum-security prisons. In the view of some people, it is fair that the violent person who is a threat to society should draw a prison sentence, while the white-collar criminal might be trusted to perform, say, a community service or some charitable work instead of going to jail. Such an alternative, it is argued, frees prison space and reduces expenses, and goes a long way toward helping rehabilitate an offender.

But, some criminals — white collar or otherwise —

will never change, no matter what kind of efforts are made to help them. Professor Schmalleger tells of a visit he once made to a prison "as an admittedly naive student of criminal justice." He asked an unrepentant inmate how he could be satisfied with his life as a burglar, and why he did not find an honest, steady job instead. The burglar threw up his hands in disgust and told Schmalleger, "Look, you and me, we live in different worlds." Schmalleger makes the valid point that most people believe the majority of convicts are people who simply fell on hard times and turned to crime. The notion, he argues, is wrong. Most convicts, he says, are professional criminals who have been socialized into lives of crime — just as we have been socialized into lives of conformity. "Because most of us don't know the criminal world, we often accept the notion that better prison facilities, more humane treatment, and stronger rehabilitation programs — all valid in their own right — will cure convicted felons of their criminal habits. But the career criminal sees himself as a legitimate professional, a view reinforced by his peculiar subculture. He is indeed a member of an 'underworld.' Perhaps it is time we recognized that there may be validity in the claim by policemen and district attorneys that most repeat offenders are criminals out of choice and not out of necessity or unhappy circumstances."[6]

That is important when we talk about treating, or rehabilitating, a criminal. We must ask ourselves: What kind of criminal are we trying to help? What sort of crimes has he or she committed? Is the crime a first offense, or just another in a long string of crimes? Should a first offender who has committed a serious crime of violence be thrown into a place where hardened, professional criminals are confined? Should we try to change the career criminal or should we simply lock him or her up, and throw away the key? Do we focus on the inmate who has gotten into trouble only once? Should more offenders be put on probation or given parole and be allowed to stay or return home?

These are difficult questions, and until we can come up with a satisfactory way of dealing with offenders, prisons, it would appear, are here to stay. They are, it seems, a prime example of a necessary evil. But this does not mean that they should be dehumanizing places. Nor should they be constant reminders of society's failures. "The degree of civilization in a society," said the Russian novelist Fëdor Dostoevski, "can be judged by entering its prisons." By that yardstick, and given the state of America's prisons, our own degree of civilization could be judged to be pretty poor. But we know, of course, that America is not a nation of Neanderthals, despite the unruly behavior of some of its citizens.

True, we do rely heavily on prisons, many of which are awful places. But our country does have the creative capacity to change them, to make them more humane places, just as we have the ability to clean up a goodly amount of the poverty and some of the other cruelties that we inflict on our neighbors. It is, however, a matter of priorities. And public offenders are not high on society's priority list. Once behind bars, they lose their rights — or so they are made to feel. They are often treated only slightly better than animals by ill-trained and unfeeling guards, many of whom, despite the uniform that gives them authority, might be locked up themselves, given their lack of regard for human feelings and their lack of knowledge about human relations.

The suggestion is not that guards in maximum-security prisons full of hard-core offenders be men afraid of their own shadows. But if reform of the prison system ever gets a higher priority, a good place to begin would be with the guards. They should be trained far better than they are now; they should be taught to work with inmates, and even about how to boost an inmate's self-worth, and not about how to keep a prisoner under control by fear and punishment.

Another step might be to reduce the size of the prisons, instead of building bigger facilities designed to warehouse more men and women. With smaller facilities, offenders could be separated according to the nature and severity of their crime, and by age; emphasis could be on determining which criminals are truly dangerous to society, and these men and women could be treated separately, and more effectively than if they were thrown in with people with totally different attitudes.

The correctional programs should be made more relevant to the outside world. For example, inmates are usually taught to make such items as birdbaths, license plates, and ashtrays, or to plant trees and repair roads. Such work has its place, but these are hardly challenging occupations. Instead, inmates could be given more opportunity to learn a truly valuable trade or profession while in prison. Libraries could be improved, medical facilities could be upgraded, and educational opportunities expanded.

But libraries, classroom instruction, and vocational training are not for everyone who enters a prison. Some men and women could not care less, no matter if they were offered free courses leading to a Ph.D., or computer training that would guarantee them a high-paying job. So, about all prison officials and criminologists can do is make rehabilitation opportunities voluntary. To sentence men or women to prison in order to rehabilitate them is as ridiculous as encouraging a teenager to hang out with hardened criminals so the teenager can learn about the seamy side of life, in order to learn what kind of behavior to avoid. But for those who wish to change, who are aware that they have made mistakes, the chance to make amends and to get a better fix on life should be there. For those who do not, punishment and confinement are the unfortunate facts of life.

In Miami, recently, the Florida House of Representatives voted to bring back the chain gang for inmates who refuse to participate in voluntary road-work programs. While it may be argued that punishing someone for *not* wanting to work is hardly the best way to make that person really *want* to work, there may be something to be said for the approach — if only that idle prisoners, like idle street gangs, are most apt to get into trouble.

About all one can say is that an option should be available, something akin to a parent who tells a teenager that he or she has to either go to school or get a job if he or she is to continue to live at home. Sometimes the options are not all that appealing to the person to whom they are offered. For those who do not accept an option there are usually consequences. The teenager who refuses to work or go to school may find himself or herself on the street if the parents are firm enough in their views. So, too, for the prison inmate. If he or she refuses to work in jail, or to learn, he or she may end up in solitary confinement, or have many privileges denied.

Whether or not the offender who refuses all help should be written off and left to rot behind bars is a question that has troubled generations of criminologists, philosophers, and social scientists. Why, after all, should a state waste money and time on someone who has no intent or desire to straighten out? Is it not the same thing as what goes on in some junior and senior high schools? We all know of students who refuse to study, who are constant pests in class, who give teachers a hard time, or who are frequently truant. Why, you might ask, should such young men and women be allowed to go to school at all? Wouldn't it be better for everyone concerned if they were simply expelled or forgotten?

It is not always that simple, or advisable. For those who see disruptive and violent behavior as diseases, like diabetes or alcoholism, there is always the possibility of a cure, or at least of lessening the symptoms. And there are those who believe that all human beings are inherently good, that given the right opportunity, goodness will overcome bad behavior.

But for many others, some criminals will always be criminals, no matter what. Moreover, those who believe that could not care less about rehabilitation, especially if they have been the victims of a violent attack, or have seen a loved one suffer the consequences of an assault. For a growing number of people today, the mounting crime and violence rate is justification enough for prisons that are not designed to rehabilitate but to lock away and punish, and to punish as harshly as possible.

The problem with that is that not all the dangerous criminals are confined. Most, in fact, are still outside, in our neighborhoods, perhaps just next door. So, if we feel safer because prisons confine, it would be well to ask, how many criminals are behind bars?

If violence is to be lessened — and that, more than punishing the offender, should be the main goal — it will not come about through confinement, because that concentrates on only the person who has been caught. If confinement cuts down the crime rate, it has yet to be proven. Prisons are convenient; they do not require much thinking about the problems of violence — not as they stand today, at least. Nor does the lack of effective aftercare for released offenders reduce the number of repeat offenders.

We suggested earlier that violent behavior is learned. Whether it can be unlearned is a difficult question. But it is doubtful that punishment will cure a violence-prone individual — nor will demeaning him or her. One can, however, at least try kindness, caring, and communication. There should be more research into the causes of violent behavior so that appropriate treatment may be applied for each case, and so that you and I will have enough information to be able to react correctly when we must consider individual situations involving a violent act. It is a mistake to lump all offenders under single labels like "psychopath," or "brain-damaged," or "convict," and treat them all the same. We must recognize that each offender is different in makeup and motives. Some, we know, will prove to be untreatable, and we must accept that. There is a vast difference between the compassion we might feel for a convict and the sentimentalism that sometimes replaces it. All those behind bars are not there because of some miscarriage of justice or damning chain of circumstantial evidence. Many belong there. But a lot of others are there because they did not get a fair hearing, or because something was not right in their lives. And many of them do want to change.

They will change if the conditions that set them on the wrong track are changed, or if the conditions they encounter in prison are improved for the better. Most important, it is wise to remember that all offenders, even the most violent, are human beings, hard as that is sometimes to appreciate. As the Project Fisherman study puts it, "Domestic stability and peace will significantly increase only when we begin to treat the public offender as an undernourished human being instead of as a failure who must be removed from the community. A democracy is dependent upon individuals being resourcefully responsible to all members of a community. To 'check' crime, we must 'check' our prisons."[7]

·8·

DEALING WITH VIOLENCE

Nothing can bring you peace but yourself.
— RALPH WALDO EMERSON

BY NOW IT SHOULD BE FAIRLY OBVIOUS to you that there are many reasons why people behave violently, and that it is very difficult to come up with an answer that will apply every time someone acts aggressively. As the French dramatist Jean Racine (1639–1699) once said: "Crime, like virtue, has its degrees." Violence, which is quite often a crime, has its degrees, too, and each shape that an act of violence takes raises its own special set of questions.

Answers to why people behave violently, however, are vital to the next questions: Can violence be prevented? And if so, how?

These questions have baffled criminologists for years, and just as there is no easy answer to the why of violent behavior, it is the same here. If by the first question we mean can violence be wiped totally away, then the answer is probably no. So long as this world is made up of different races, religions, cultures, and political philosophies, violence will never disappear; there will always be despots who will use violence to get what they want, and there will always be saviors who will use violence to prevent tyrants from using more of it. Past history certainly tells us that aggressive acts are as much a part of this world as other forms of human behavior. If angels and kings, and God himself can engage in it, are we to be holier than they? Indeed, it has been suggested that if God had not given us violence, it would have shown a flaw in his power, for it would have meant he could not do everything.

The future, too, at least the foreseeable one, shows clearly that violence and the tools of violence are not going to go away. One does not have to look, once again, beyond the daily news to see that: nuclear weapons are being made more and more powerful and are being acquired by more nations; personal weapons are as common as automobiles and as easily bought or stolen.

Nevertheless, despite that gloomy outlook and despite the fact that abolition of violence is an unrealistic and idealistic goal, violence can be lessened.

But how?

Prison is one way. But as was shown in the previous chapter, it is not always the best way. Indeed, imprisonment, especially under inhuman conditions that focus more on punishment than on rehabilitation, further degrades the offender who is still, after all, a human being, and may worsen his or her antisocial behavior. It is true that some men and women seem to change their attitude

for the better behind bars. But there is no guarantee
that when they are freed they will "go straight," least of
all if whatever it was that put them in jail to begin
with — social conditions, psychiatric problems, or brain
chemicals and chromosomes gone wrong — is still
present. In fact, the vast majority of people arrested in
any year have a prior record.

Part of the blame must lie with society, which is generally reluctant to rehabilitate an ex-convict. It is a
common view that people who commit crimes must be
punished, not helped, and that punishment, while it may
not always deter those who have committed one crime
already, goes a long way toward scaring off others who
might believe they can get away with a crime.

Punishment, of course, has its place. The law must be
upheld if we are to avoid utter chaos, and punishment is
an important way of making people abide by the law.
As the German philosopher Friedrich Nietzsche
(1844–1900) put it, "The broad effects which can be
obtained by punishment in man and beast are the increase of fear, the sharpening of the sense of cunning,
the mastery of the desires; so it is that punishment
tames man but does not make him 'better.' " Capital
punishment, too, despite the controversy that swirls
around it, has long been regarded as a right of the state.
In fact, the death penalty seems to be sanctioned by the
Bible (Genesis 9:6): "Whoso sheddeth man's blood, by
man shall his blood be shed. . . ."

Sometimes, we punish too little. This can often happen simply because there is no one to punish. "For one
thing," *Time* magazine reported in a special issue on
violence,

the majority of criminals go untouched by the [American criminal justice system]. The police learn about one-quarter of the thefts committed each year, and about less than half the robberies, burglaries and rapes. Either victims are afraid or ashamed to report crimes, or they may conclude gloomily that nothing will be done if they do. Murder is the crime police do hear about, but only 73 percent of the nation's murders lead to arrest. The arrest rates for lesser crimes are astonishingly low — 59 percent for aggravated assault in 1979, 48 percent for rape, 25 percent for robbery, 15 percent for burglary.

Even when a suspect is apprehended, the chances of his getting punished are mighty slim. In New York State each year there are some 130,000 felony arrests; approximately 8,000 people go to prison. There are 94,000 felony arrests in New York City; 5,000 to 6,000 serve time. A 1974 study of the District of Columbia came up with a similar picture. Of those arrested for armed robbery, less than one-quarter went to prison. More than 6,000 aggravated assaults were reported; 116 people were put away.[1]

Violent juveniles, too, are rarely punished, even when they are convicted of an offense that would put an adult in jail for life. Rather, if they are under eighteen years of age, they are tried in juvenile courts, usually in secret; the records are sealed and not made public. All of this is done out of a long-standing tradition that tries to protect minors from a public trial and the hard light of publicity that might leave some psychic scar.

There has been a recent move in some states, however, to try in an adult court juveniles accused of violent crimes. A few years ago, Senator Edward M. Kennedy (Democrat, Massachusetts) argued that juvenile courts had failed, and that "some significant punishment" should be imposed on the young offender who commits a violent crime. "There has been a notorious lack of rehabilitation," Kennedy said. "The violent juvenile is often let off with a slap on the wrist. Age cannot justify treating the seventeen-year-old rapist or murderer differently from his adult counterpart. The poor, the black, the elderly — those most often victimized by crime — do not make such distinctions. Nor should the courts."[2]

Sometimes, criminals go unpunished because the court dockets are full, and some prosecutors with heavy case loads may want to press only those cases that will not take too long or that may be won easily. At other times, because they are overworked, both prosecutors and police get careless, and begin to miss clues, keep sloppy records, and fail to ask the right questions. And there are times when the justice system itself, often so intent on protecting the criminal that it neglects the victim, is to blame for not punishing when it should. Syndicated columnist William Raspberry recently addressed such an issue in the case of Jack Ronald Jones, a twenty-six-year-old man convicted of the kidnap, repeated rape, and premeditated murder of a Maryland college honor student. Jones had not only raped the young woman but had also beaten her with a chain, shot her in the head when she tried to escape and, finally, set her body afire. Although Maryland law provides for the death penalty for murder and rape, the jury found there were "mitigating" circumstances — that is, circumstances that made the crimes seem less harsh — that did not justify death for Jones. The prison term he was given instead made him eligible for parole in twelve years. Wrote Raspberry, "There were mitigating circumstances in this ghastly kidnap, murder, torture, rape and mutilation? Incredibly, the jury said there were. Jones had cooperated with the police after his arrest. His harsh upbringing as a child had contributed to his behavior. He was unlikely to pose a threat to society in the future, presumably because he had sought religious counseling, and he was remorseful. Further, the jury found, Jones' use of drugs may have contributed to this heinous crime. And, finally, his execution would have meant lifelong anguish for his immediate family, including his wife and six-year-old son."[3]

It is not unnatural for us to want to punish a criminal severely in such cases. But, unfortunately, we often confuse punishing a criminal for flouting the law with revenge. Although the two are closely related, there is a difference. Punishment is — or should be — a penalty imposed for violating the law. It is usually handed down by some authority. It can be meted out by a court, acting for the people, when the court fines or sentences a criminal to prison; it can be ordered by a congressional committee when that committee censures a member of Congress for misconduct; it can be the right of a company, which fires an employee for stealing or for not performing his or her job; it is the army or navy handing out a dishonorable discharge to a soldier or sailor who does not abide by the service's rules and regulations; it can be a mother or father who takes away a child's allowance or forbids him or her to go out. Revenge, on the other hand, is the inflicting of punishment, but usually by groups or individuals who do not have the authority to punish; it is generally the result of hatred rather than justice; it is returning injury for injury to obtain satisfaction, often for personal reasons. Thus, revenge can be unjust punishment.

The problem is that many times even those allowed by law to punish do so out of vengeance. Says one authority on the subject:

> Men seek revenge because they feel that their rights or interests have been encroached upon. The act of revenge is one strictly of self-defense, and is primarily a reflex action. It seeks to destroy or render powerless what constitutes a menace, but it contains a rough notion of justice, of the idea that no one can intrude upon the rights of another without suffering the consequences. The exercise of justice by a community or its representatives against an individual who is obnoxious to it, or to any of its members, is based primarily on the feeling which underlies revenge. Punishment is to some extent vengeance — the vengeance of society for its own preservation. The criminal must suffer, must expiate his crime, whatever other notions may in time enter into the idea of punishment. Private vengeance and public justice are thus so far similar in their point of view and in their action, save that the latter tends to be more discriminating and impartial.[4]

Since private desires for revenge often exist side by side with punishment handed out by a court or another form of authority, it is easy to see how a jury, say, might misuse its authority and inflict cruel and unusual punishment on a criminal out of anger. And when this is done, it generally means that the judgment against a criminal has been made more severe because the criminal violated someone's idea of morality rather than any specific law. Again, a crime can be so horrid that revenge is on everyone's mind and, as noted, this is understandable. Probably every one of us has wanted to hurt someone who hurt us, and many of us have gone out of our way to injure that person, either physically or emotionally. How much effort we put into hurting somebody else, how much force we use, usually depends on how much hurt has been done to us. Under such circumstances, we feel justified in saying that the person who injured us got just what he or she deserved.

But this kind of reasoning condemns the offender more than the offense, the sinner more than the sin. It also means giving up on the offender, saying, in effect, that he or she is not to be helped, or cannot be changed. Condemning the individual, in the view of some criminologists, also avoids placing responsibility on factors other than the individual. "The psychiatrist's way of thinking about criminal responsibility has a social as well as an individual aspect," writes one commentator on crime and punishment. "He would argue, for example, that the slum is to the offender what the polluted well is to the typhoid case. In the fixing of criminal responsibility, in the psychiatric sense — that is, in the determination of who and what must change — the slum as well as the individual offender must be incriminated."[5]

It is one thing to blame society, but certainly not as

easy to actually punish it. So, judges usually have little alternative but to put the criminal away for as long a time as the law allows, and as long a time as possible to protect society. And, as has been pointed out, once a person is behind bars, chances are not too good that he or she will come out a better person for it.

So, until better ways of rehabilitating the hardened criminal are found, about all society can do is try to reduce crime by preventing people from becoming criminals in the first place, and by taking other steps to make crimes difficult to commit, either by repeat offenders or by new ones.

An obvious way of stopping many people from turning into criminals is to wipe out slums, improve living conditions, provide jobs and more recreational facilities. But social reform costs money. And, unfortunately, it is sometimes not a priority of politicians, who ignore the key role the environment plays in causing crime and violence. They certainly are aware that poor neighborhoods breed violence, but these places are often written off as a simple fact of urban life; sometimes, politicians ignore urban ghettos because they do not live there themselves, at other times they honestly believe the money spent there would be wasted.

Those who feel that cleaning up slums is an impractical way of dealing with crime often lean toward sterner laws. Over the years, all kinds of crime-fighting packages have been submitted to Congress, to state legislatures, and to city and town officials. Few call for improving the environment. Instead, they call for a variety of other remedies: easier ways to convict a criminal, more prisons, tranquilizing prisoners with calming drugs, forcing murderers to support the families of victims, making murder by a hired gunman a federal rather than a state offense, mandatory prison terms for any crime involving the use of a gun or other deadly weapon, banning handguns, denying bail to violent criminals, admitting illegally obtained information as evidence in criminal cases, more surveillance of citizens' activities, more restrictions on citizens' movements, more detailed files on how citizens behave, making it harder for a criminal to win parole from prison, cracking down on the right to appeal, and making it more difficult for a killer to plead insanity, thus sending more murderers to prison rather than to mental hospitals.

It should be apparent that some of these suggestions would do little more than put an extra load on already crowded courtroom calendars, or add to the population of prisons now filled to the bursting point. Others of these suggestions might endanger the civil rights of the accused, presume guilt too quickly, and punish too hastily; civil rights of the ordinary citizen might also be violated if people who have committed no crime are observed too carefully, or their movements restricted by government authorities more interested in law and order than in what they might regard as "high-minded principles." Examine each of the foregoing suggestions carefully, discussing their pros and cons in light of what you have read in the previous chapters. Bear in mind that the balance between preserving the rights of the accused on the one hand and those of the victim on the other is a delicate one. Each has rights, and emphasizing one over the other is sure to provoke heated debate. Some argue that society fails to provide adequate protection for law-abiding citizens while it overemphasizes safeguards for the accused and for convicted criminals. Others argue that law-abiding citizens would understand the rights of some accused better if they themselves were under suspicion for something they did not do; this view holds that if one is to err it is best to err on the side of protecting the accused rather than to make a mistake and imprison or execute him or her unjustly.

But no matter which side of the argument one leans on, it is difficult to ignore the violence that seems to be everywhere today. And it becomes increasingly harder for us to let the criminals go unpunished. "Are we not hostages within the borders of our own self-styled enlightened, civilized country?" asked U.S. Chief Justice Warren Burger recently. "Accurate figures on the cost of home burglar alarms, of three locks on each door — and, sadly, of handgun sales for householders — are not available but they run into hundreds of millions of dollars. All this in a 'civilized,' 'enlightened' society."[6]

There is no question that Americans are afraid. They fear the city streets, especially after dark; they fear the parks, once places to play and relax; they are afraid in their own homes, once sacred places where few who were not invited came and that today are a challenge to the burglar or the rapist, who is quite capable of injuring or killing the occupants; Americans even are afraid to purchase an over-the-counter medication because every so often some deranged person will poison the medicines; and they are afraid to send their children out to trick-or-treat because, again, someone with a warped mind may put razor blades in the Halloween apples.

The depth to which that fear can run was perhaps best seen in the recent murders and suspected murders of a number of black children in Atlanta, Georgia. While the police and the FBI worked to catch the murderer (a young man was finally caught and convicted of killing two of the children), psychologists and social workers became concerned about the mental health of the children living in the area. Most of the children, it was discovered, had become anxious and fearful. Among the symptoms they displayed: bed-wetting, fighting in school, nightmares, lower test scores, clinging to parents, making tiny rather than large human figures in drawings (an indication of a lack of self-confidence). Many of the children slept with Bibles or toys for protection. One adult wrote to the Atlanta *Journal-Constitution:* "I have two five-year-old girls who were playing with their dolls. One doll was pretending to lure the other with a promise of french fries. The other doll declared, very matter-of-factly, 'You might strangle me.' "[7]

So strong was the impact of the murders, said the psychologists, that the children's capacity to trust, love, and be independent was in danger of being permanently impaired. "At such young ages," commented Atlanta psychiatrist Alfred Messer, "children should be experimenting with the world, having a romance with it. Now they are forced into passivity and inhibition, and prevented from being adventuresome. They must always be with one adult. If this goes on much longer, we are breeding a whole generation of children who grow up choosing dependency as a primary tool for coping with life's stresses."[8]

Because of the emotional damage that the fear of violence can cause, it is not surprising that so many people take a hard-line stand with respect to dealing with criminals and when talking about how to prevent crime. After John W. Hinckley, Jr., was found innocent by reason of insanity in attempting to kill President Reagan and injuring three other men, the decision to confine him to a mental ward created a furor. Many authorities called for a tightening of the rules for an insanity defense, and some would have abolished it completely, a move that would have been unfair to individuals who have such a serious mental illness that they are totally unable to appreciate the wrongfulness of their conduct. But there is no perfect test for insanity, and it is often quite difficult, perhaps impossible, to determine whether a person who behaves violently is too crazy for prison or too sane for a mental hospital. Psychiatry is still a very inexact science, and psychiatrists still cannot accurately predict who will become a violent criminal. Until they do, society cannot rely on mental tests to help reduce or prevent violence. And even if we could, would filling all our jails and mental hospitals with potential criminals and the criminally insane solve our problems?

So, once again, we are faced with that thorny question: How does one go about slowing up the violence that has infected society? There are two possible solutions left. One of them, strict gun control, is a tangible, attainable approach. The other, reeducating society to shun violence, is idealistic, perhaps naive, but not out of the question. Let's look first at gun control.

To say that guns are everywhere is no overstatement. We see them dangling at the hips of policemen, in the closets of dads who hunt, in the hands of terrorists and gangsters, sheriffs and cowboys in the movies and on TV; guns are hanging over fireplaces or locked in display cases to be admired; they are copied in wood and plastic and steel and called toys. Guns are fired at targets to demonstrate skill and sharp eyes, and into the air at a military funeral or to start a sporting event; often, they are fired in anger, or out of fear or some uncontrollable urge, at people. These guns do not include the heavier weapons mounted on the tanks, planes, and ships of the world's armies, navies, and air forces; nor do they include the weapons carried by soldiers and marines in battle. We are concerned here with the revolvers and the automatics, the handguns that have become so common in America and that are too often used to kill or maim another human being.

It is estimated that there are fifty million privately owned handguns in the United States alone. People own them for many reasons: for personal protection, for target practice, as collectors' items — and to terrorize. Since most of the owners are men, it has been suggested that such guns are a macho prop, a symbol of the sort of manhood associated with the tough frontiersmen of the Old West. Perhaps this is true in some cases, especially when guns are never or rarely fired. More to the point, though, is that handguns, which are fairly easy to obtain and easier still to hide on one's person, figure prominently in the many murders recorded every year in the United States. Those who wish to control the manufacture, sale, and possession of handguns argue that although knives and clubs, for instance, may be used to kill someone, they require more effort and may not do the job as quickly as a gun; it is a very simple matter to pull a trigger, and chances are that in the heat of anger a person with a gun in hand will kill more readily than with a knife or some other weapon. Said New York City's chief of detectives, James T. Sullivan, "The most effective means of decreasing homicide would be to have extensive layoffs in the gun-manufacturing industry."[9] Chief Sullivan had good reason for his remark — nearly 60 percent of the murders in the city in 1981 were committed with handguns.

Although it may be argued that strong gun-control laws will not automatically reduce the violent crime rate — no more than Prohibition stopped people from drinking — it is difficult to ignore the fact that as long as hundguns are easily obtainable the crime rate is not going to go down. Even the noncriminal, the average person who has never fired a gun before, might be more apt to shoot to kill, not only in self-defense but out of rage, if a gun were close by.

There is also the intriguing suggestion that the very sight of a handgun may be enough to stimulate someone into behaving more violently than he or she had intended; just as the Russian physiologist Ivan Pavlov caused dogs to salivate when he rang a bell, so, too, may a handgun act as a stimulus to aggression. Someone who has studied this phenomenon is Dr. Leonard Berkowitz, a professor of psychology at the University of Wisconsin, and an authority on aggression. In one of his studies, a group of students was asked to come up with ideas that would help the record sales and popularity of a popular singer. Each student was assigned a partner who would supposedly evaluate the ideas. Then Dr. Berkowitz explained to the students that if the partner thought the ideas were good, he or she would apply a mild electric shock with a machine to the student; if the idea was considered poor, up to ten shocks would be given. As the experiment progressed, it turned out that half of the subjects got one shock each from their partners, the other half got seven each. Now, it was assumed that those who got the seven shocks would be quite angry, both because of the pain and because their ideas were rated poorly.

Next, Dr. Berkowitz had the subjects trade places with their partners, and then divided them into three groups. On the table where the first group sat was the telegraph key to administer the shocks; for the second group, the table also had badminton rackets and shuttlecocks on it; for the third, a shotgun and a revolver were placed alongside the telegraph key. "We then showed the subjects a list of ideas presumably compiled by the partner and asked them to judge the list and deliver the appropriate number of shocks," Berkowitz reported.

As we suspected, the presence of the guns affected both the number of shocks the students gave their partners and the length of time they held the key down for each shock. From a statistical point of view, our most significant finding was that when the angry subjects saw the guns, they gave more shocks than any other group.

On the basis of this and related research, I argued that a weapon could function as a conditioned stimulus, eliciting reactions that were associated with the object. Thus, if people already think of a rifle or pistol (or a knife or even a club) as something that is used to hurt others deliberately, then the mere sight of the weapon can evoke in them both the ideas and motor responses they associate with aggression. Further, should the people be disposed to attack someone at the time — as were our angry group of students — the stimulus of the weapon could strengthen whatever open aggression they are inclined to display.

Concluded Berkowitz, "The implication of the argument is clear. I contended, and still contend, that we sometimes react mindlessly and impulsively to the presence of guns. Since that is so, the more control the law exercises over the availability of guns, the better."[10]

Berkowitz has also pointed out that the extent of this "weapons effect" is suggested by several studies that have noticed a rise in aggressive behavior among children playing with toy guns or other aggression-associated toys. In two similar studies, researchers watched children aged four and five in a nursery school for several weeks. Sometimes, the children had their usual toys; at other times, they were given toys like airplanes; in other sessions, they got toy guns. "In both studies," said Berkowitz, "play with the toy guns led to a higher rate of antisocial behavior — pushing, shoving, hitting — than occurred on the average with airplanes or other toys. Children, too, it seems, associate guns with aggression and act accordingly."[11]

Not everyone agrees that guns should be banned, or their ownership restricted. Even President Reagan, wounded by an assassin, has opposed gun control in favor of stiff mandatory jail terms for those who use a gun to commit a crime. At a recent news conference, the President was asked if things would have been different if John Hinckley had had more difficulty getting a gun. The President replied, "Hinckley did what he did in an area that has the strictest gun control laws that there are in the United States. Now, how effective are gun control laws for someone that wants to commit a crime using a gun when he could choose the place where they're supposed to be least likely to have one?" In an editorial, the *New York Times* responded by agreeing that those laws, to be sure, are not very effective — but for a reason that the President chose not to emphasize. Said the *Times,* "Local gun control laws aren't much good if people are free to buy weapons elsewhere."[12]

The National Rifle Association, most powerful of the gun lobbies in America, maintains that it is not guns that kill people, it is people who do so Those who strongly oppose gun control argue that if a person really wants to kill someone, he or she will find a way to do it anyway, no matter how many laws are passed. Moreover, they say, it would be virtually impossible to collect all the guns now in circulation. Nor would that be fair, say opponents of control, because guns have many recreational uses, and they also enable people living in high-crime areas to protect themselves. "Punish those who misuse firearms, but leave me alone," is the way Lafe Pfeifer, secretary of the Texas State Rifle Association, has put it.[13]

Finally, there is the position that the Second Amendment of the U.S. Constitution allows us to have guns: "A well-regulated militia, being necessary to the security of a free state, the right of the people to keep and bear arms, shall not be infringed."

Each of the arguments has merit, although the last — the constitutional right to bear arms — is on shaky ground. Courts have held that the right must have some reasonable relationship to a well-regulated federal militia, a term applied to citizens subject to U.S. military service in an emergency. It is stretching the point to suggest that handguns in the possession of everyone who wants one are covered by the Second Amendment.

Perhaps stronger gun laws will not put an end to murder, and perhaps some of the pro-gun lobbyists have a good case. But gun laws are certainly better than nothing. If a person knows he or she will be fined heavily or put in jail for a long time if caught with a handgun, there is a chance that person may not carry one. And where there is no gun, the chance of a violent crime taking place is considerably lessened. Wrote columnist Adam Smith, "The hard work is not just to get the gunners to join in; the hard work is to do something about our ragged system of criminal justice, to shore up our declining faith in the institutions that are supposed to protect us, and to promote the notion that people should take the responsibility for their own actions."[14]

That last point, that people should be responsible for their own actions, leads us to the last possible solution to slowing the pattern of violence — reeducating society. As stated before it is perhaps a naive approach, but not out of the question. Changing people's attitudes *is* difficult, and that goes for changing the public's attitude toward crime and violence. Unfortunately, although most people become incensed when a crime is directed against them or against someone they know, they cool rather quickly, and soon forget. Many people also condone certain criminal activities, either because they feel everybody commits them, or because they believe the person against whom a particular assault, say, is directed deserved it. That last sentiment was expressed, in fact, in a study published in *Psychology Today* magazine. University of California sociologists James McEvoy and Rodney Stark polled more than a thousand adult Americans in an effort to learn whether Americans are violent people. The answers they received indicated that one out of five Americans believes that "some politicians who have their lives threatened probably deserve it"; and one American in eleven agreed that "sometimes I have felt that the best thing for our country might be the death of some of our political leaders."

Noting that the responses indicated that a substantial minority of Americans, far from being horrified by political assassination, tacitly condone it, the researchers observed, "In fact, many Americans seem resigned to assassinations as a fact of our political life. A majority,

55 percent, agree that 'politicians who try to change things too fast have to expect that their lives may be threatened.' " The study also disclosed:

- Half of the respondents agreed that "justice may have been a little rough and ready in the days of the Old West, but things worked better than they do now with all the legal red tape."
- One American in four believes that groups have the right to train their members in marksmanship and underground warfare tactics "in order to help put down any conspiracies that might occur in the country."
- One American in five approves of slapping one's spouse on appropriate occasions. Surprisingly, the researchers found that approval of this practice increases with income and education.
- One American in ten would physically assault antiwar demonstrators who blocked rush-hour traffic.

Views like that, which might be justified in some circumstances, strengthen the belief of many psychologists and sociologists that violence is deeply rooted in our values. It is true that as times change, so do people's attitudes toward many things. For example, polls taken during wartime might indicate that people would be more apt to condone violence then than during peacetime; in peak periods of crime, more people might believe that it would be right to kill both in self-defense and for revenge; during times of social unrest, people might feel easier about using violence to effect change, or deadly force to stop those who would bring about change.

The fact remains that for too many people violence is

an acceptable action and reaction, just as many people believe that the worst thing about crime is getting caught. As mentioned in the chapter on group violence, the mobster is often idolized, a fact that makes many of us wonder whether we really care about the way criminals behave. As Mark Furstenburg of the International Association of Chiefs of Police has put it:

> Organized crime depends not on victims, but on customers. All its activities depend on establishment of a long-term, continuing relationship between criminal and customer, who share criminal responsibility, and therefore have an equal stake in thwarting the police. Gambling is illegal; yet millions of Americans want to gamble regularly. Operation of many popular kinds of gambling requires an elaborate, expensive organization, with personnel, places of business, wire services, capital, and a national organization which can corrupt to keep itself safe. Sale of narcotics is illegal, and yet [thousands] of Americans want heroin regularly. The manufacture, importation, and sale of hard narcotics is a huge enterprise, requiring overseas operations, professional smuggling, and a large processing and sales organization. Organized crime can provide it. Who else could? Usury is a crime, but there are thousands of Americans — businessmen, consumers, gamblers — who need short-term credit without references, collateral, or questions. Loansharking requires a capital investment, sizable personnel, and enforcement powers. Organized crime can provide these things. As long as Americans enact their consciences, and live their tastes, organized crime will be needed.[15]

And violence, too, will continue to thrive as long as violence is glorified, as long as the capacity to destroy someone or something is treated with near reverence by the media and by government leaders who lack faith in any other way of solving domestic and international problems. "If violence still persists," said psychologist Benjamin B. Wolman, a specialist in group tensions, some years ago, "it must be viewed as a dated, obsolete method of dealing with social ills. Since it does not promote the survival of a society, it is anticultural. Any society which fosters the use of violence as a method of solution for inner conflicts suffers from deculturation. If humanity will permit conflicts to lead to international violence, the process of deculturation will clearly become suicidal."[16]

Dr. Wolman, who was addressing a meeting of the American Association for the Advancement of Science, then asked what a group of scholars and scientists could do about violence. Admitting he had no pat solutions, he remarked:

> We can't stop armies in combat, but we can influence parents and teachers, newspapermen and movie producers and point out their potential role in preventing homicide and suicide. We can counteract the license that sweeps our cities. We can reeducate parents and teachers toward assuming moral responsibility for their children rather than appeasing, bribing and demoralizing them. . . . There is little gain, if any, by swinging the pendulum from a too restrictive education to no education whatsoever, from exaggerated parental and teacher authority to the renunciation of educational responsibility. Even cats and dogs brought up together can be educated not to hate one another; can't we accomplish the same thing with human beings? Why must children be brought up to

compete with one another? Why must boys be encouraged to be aggressive, tough guys and bullies? If there is innate drive toward aggressive behavior, it must be controlled, channelled and sublimated. There is no reason for following the so-called natural drives; we do not eliminate and urinate in public as animals do. We build sewage systems to protect our physical health; how about sewage canals for our mental health?[17]

Dr. Wolman called on scientists to unravel the causes of conflicts, discover the factors that aggravate them, and then work out ways to alleviate group tensions and to possibly resolve conflicts. "Our knowledge of human nature and interpersonal relations need not be restricted to our clinics and laboratories," he declared. "We must embark upon a large scale research program with the aim of promoting mutual understanding of the various classes, races, and nations toward the protection of human lives and survival of the human race."[18]

The second task, Wolman said, is directed toward the education process at home and in school. "Children gifted in mathematics must not be taught how to score easy victories over their less fortunate classmates. Children must be taught to help one another and not compete with each other. We must educate our children to respect the one who shares, who helps, and who cares, instead of the dubious hero of violence. We must work toward revamping our entire educational philosophy, toward directing children's initiative and energy, toward constructive goals, toward admiration of creativity, productivity and cooperation versus the glorification of the pseudo power of destruction and violence."[19]

We must also educate society. Earlier, we suggested

that one thing that contributed to violence and crime was a poor environment. If that is so, then it stands to reason that improving the quality of people's lives, offering them more opportunity and rewards for constructive activity, more ways to melt away some of their aggressions, and even money, would be a valuable way to lessen antisocial and violent behavior. That last, money, may indeed be the root of all evil — but there is no doubting that it also reduces poverty and, thus, in many instances the need to commit some violent act to get it. Money also makes people comfortable, usually happy. And just knowing that money and success are attainable is encouraging to someone who might otherwise lose all hope and resort to criminal activity, even violence, to obtain what most of us want.

Moreover, people influence one another. The more happy, motivated, and comfortable people are, the more they will inspire others. It is when only a few are happy, when only a handful share the wealth, that things heat up — be it the political climate of a poverty-stricken country where a minority of privileged people control its destiny, or an urban slum thriving across the tracks from an affluent neighborhood — and violence breaks out. Reward is always much better than punishment. When it is bestowed for a job well done or a thought well conceived, it pays huge dividends. And make no mistake about it, unfavorable social conditions are a form of punishment in the sense that they represent rough and severe treatment of people. As was seen in our discussion of the social causes of violence and delinquency, such conditions injure one's self-concept.

Self-concepts are very hard to change, but educators know that they can be changed by experiences that mean something to the individual. People must be constantly reassured that they have worth and value; their work should be praised when it merits praise; their ideas should be heeded and discussed, whether they are naive or worldly.

Violent behavior, in the last analysis, comes from within. It makes no difference whether it is guns or groups or genes, slums or psychosis, that touch it off. What is important is the realization that violence, ultimately, is an individual act. Someone must pull the trigger, someone plants the terrorist bomb, someone batters a child or a spouse, or rapes a woman. Blaming society in general, or "heredity," for aggression is not only quite understandable but valid, for they do play roles in causing violence. To lessen it if not stop it, however, we must concentrate on the individual. If indeed there is a relationship between brain abnormalities and murder, then more research and more clinical examinations of potentially violent individuals should be done. There must be a better understanding of the difference between who is the dangerous person and who is the mentally ill one because the two do not always go together. Too often, the emotionally disturbed are considered potentially dangerous even though their illness will never drive them to commit a criminal act.

On the other hand, we also quite often ignore the signs of a potentially dangerous person because he or she has never been in trouble with the law, or because he or she comes from a "good family." We must learn to look for the signs of the violence-prone individual, subtle as they are sometimes, and to consider the possibility that he or she might commit a violent act. The friend or neighbor who is always aggressive when he has had too much to drink, the person who always seems to be at odds with society, the young man who treats women harshly, who has a chip on his shoulder, who sees himself as worthless, or who hangs with the wrong crowd or with no crowd at all — all of these people could and often do turn violent.

Not everyone who demonstrates such symptoms is going to murder or maim. And although you cannot and should not suspect every single personality quirk, it is always good to give instances of odd behavior a quick glance over the shoulder every so often. It is wise to always be alert to the possibility.

Dr. John Monahan, professor of law, psychology, and legal medicine at the University of Virginia, put it appropriately before a 1982 meeting of the American Psychiatric Association. In place of the simple statement that psychiatrists and psychologists cannot predict violence, he suggested instead that mental health professionals ought to adopt the following dictum: "Little is known about how accurately violent behavior can be predicted in many circumstances, but it may be possible to predict it accurately enough to be useful in some policy decisions."[20]

None of you are yet psychologists or psychiatrists. Some of you will be one day. But for now, we must all be alert to the people around us — but more than that, to be tuned in to our own personalities as closely as possible. We must examine our own feelings, our own attitudes, our own responses to certain situations. Do we feel violence is justified? If so, when? If not, what is the alternative? Do we have a tendency to react belligerently when things do not go our way? Do we resort to physical means to make a point? Do we try to control our emotions, or do we explode regularly? When we are assaulted or insulted, do we do as Mohandas K. Gandhi, India's great nationalist leader, did and turn the other cheek? Do we, as he did, view nonviolence as the highest goal, the wisest course a human being can seek? In his words, "Nonviolence is the first article of my faith. It is also the last article of my creed."

Gandhi died, as have so many men who rejected violence, at the hands of an assassin. And so, too, did another peaceful man, the Reverend Martin Luther King, Jr. When he received the Nobel Peace Prize on December 11, 1964, he said something about aggression and nonviolence that bears remembering and is an uplifting end to a book that has had to dwell at times on some rather bleak realities. "Nonviolence," he said, "is the answer to the crucial political and moral questions of our time; the need for man to overcome oppression and violence without resorting to oppression and violence. Man must evolve for all human conflict a method which rejects revenge, aggression and retaliation. The foundation of such a method is love."

NOTES

INTRODUCTION

1. "Toward a New Language," *Saturday Review,* May 24, 1969, p. 24.
2. Dena Kleiman, "In Third Grade, Violence Is Put in Perspective," *New York Times,* April 7, 1981, p. B3.
3. "Fearful Americans," *Discover,* November 1980, p. 14.

CHAPTER I

1. "Aggression in Captive Groups of Rhesus Macaques," *Primate News* (Oregon Regional Primate Research Center, Beaverton, Oregon), p. 1.
2. Annie Dillard, *A Pilgrim at Tinker's Creek* (New York: Harper's Magazine Press, 1974), pp. 63–64.
3. *The Social Contract* (New York: Atheneum, 1970), p. 286.
4. *International Encyclopedia of the Social Sciences,* Vol. 1 (New York: Macmillan, 1968), p. 168.
5. "Ritualized Fighting," in *The Natural History of Aggression* (New York: Academic Press, 1964), p. 49.
6. *Aggression and Crimes of Violence* (New York: Oxford University Press, 1975), p. 5.

7. Lynn Gillis, *Human Behaviour in Illness* (London: Faber and Faber, 1980), pp. 36–37.

8. News release, University of Southern California, May 15, 1978.

9. Ibid.

10. *Crimes of Violence,* staff report submitted to the National Commission on the Causes and Prevention of Violence (Washington, D.C.: U.S. Government Printing Office, 1969), p. xxxii.

11. Ramsey Clark, *Crime in America* (New York: Simon and Schuster, 1970), p. 57.

12. Leonard Buder, "Almost 25 Percent of Homicides in City in '81 Tied to Drugs," *New York Times,* p. B1.

13. "Debunking Ideas on Teen Troubles," *San Francisco Chronicle,* August 30, 1982, p. 2.

14. John Langone, "The Lennon Syndrome," *Discover,* February 1981, p. 75.

15. Loretta McLaughlin, "Boston Doctors Tell How to Spot the Violent Ones in Advance," *Boston Herald,* March 26, 1967, p. 31.

16. *Violence and the Brain* (New York: Harper and Row, 1970), p. 4.

17. Ibid.

18. Ibid.

19. News release, American Medical Association, July 23, 1982.

20. "Aggressive Behavior: The Hormonal Input," *Science News,* March 14, 1981, p. 166.

21. News release, American Academy of Pediatrics, July 1, 1974.

22. Bayard Webster, "Health Chief Cites Rise in Violent Deaths of Young," *New York Times,* October 27, 1982.

23. "Television and Growing Up: The Impact of Televised Violence," Report to the Surgeon General, from the Surgeon General's Scientific Advisory Committee on Television and Social Behavior, National Institute of Mental Health, Rockville, Maryland, 1972, p. 11.

24. News release, American Academy of Pediatrics, July 1, 1974.

25. *Clinical Psychiatry News,* March 1981, p. 16.

26. Ibid.

27. *Christian Science Monitor,* February 3, 1981, p. B6.

28. Ibid.

29. "Bloodbaths Debase Movies and Audiences," *New York Times,* November 21, 1982, p. 1H.

30. *Clinical Psychiatry News,* May 1980, p. 25.

31. News release, University of Texas at Austin, October 17, 1980.

32. Lois Entwisle, June 22, 1982, p. A8.

CHAPTER II

1. R. L. Sutherland and Julian L. Woodward, *Introductory Sociology,* 2nd edition (Philadelphia: J. B. Lippincott, 1940), p. 317.

2. "Is Mass Violence an Epidemic Disease?," *Medical World News,* September 1, 1967, p. 48.

3. Joe Eszterhas and Michael D. Roberts, *Thirteen Seconds: Confrontation at Kent State* (New York: Dodd, Mead & Co., 1970), pp. 163, 8.

4. *New York Times,* September 16, 1971, p. 1.

5. "Is Mass Violence an Epidemic Disease?," *Medical World News,* September 1, 1967, p. 48.

6. Ibid, p. 45.

7. Richard F. Raper, *The Tragedy of Lynching* (Chapel Hill: University of North Carolina Press, 1933), p. 5.

8. Ibid, p. 7.

9. Ibid, p. 12.

10. "Violations in El Salvador Unabated," *Nation's Health,* February 1983, p. 1.

11. *New York Times,* February 8, 1983, p. A18.

12. George McKnight, *The Terrorist Mind* (Indianapolis: Bobbs-Merrill, 1974), p. 181.

13. Edgar O'Ballance, *Language of Violence* (San Rafael, Calif.: Presidio Press, 1979), p. 4.
14. Haguromo Society, *Born to Die*, February 1, 1952.
15. Charles William Heckethorn, *The Secret Societies of All Ages and Countries*, Vol. 1 (New York: University Books, 1965), p. 176.
16. Ibid, p. 181.
17. Stanley F. Horn, *Invisible Empire* (Boston: Houghton Mifflin, 1939), p. 1.
18. Ibid, p. 86.
19. Ibid, pp. 376–377.
20. Task Force Report, Organized Crime, President's Commission on Law Enforcement and Administration of Justice, 1967, p. 1.
21. Ibid, p. 925.
22. Ibid, p. 925.
23. Ibid, p. 925.
24. Henry Kamm, "Pope Begins Visit to Mafia Stronghold," *New York Times,* November 21, 1982, p. 8.
25. Task Force Report, Organized Crime, President's Commission on Law Enforcement and Administration of Justice, 1967, p. 27, Appendix A.
26. Ibid, p. 27
27. Ibid, p. 3.

CHAPTER III

1. "Assassination and Political Violence" in *A Report to the National Commission on the Causes and Prevention of Violence,* Vol. 8 (October 1969), p. 10.
2. "The Assassination Syndrome," reprinted in *Annual Editions: Criminal Justice* (Guilford, Conn.: Dushkin Publishing, 1982), p. 37 (from *Saturday Evening Post,* October 1981).

3. "Assassination and Political Violence," p. 54.

4. P. Wallechinsky and I. Wallace, *The People's Almanac*, No. 3 (New York: William Morrow, 1981), p. 48.

5. "The Assassination Syndrome," reprinted in *Annual Editions: Criminal Justice* (Guilford, Conn.: Dushkin Publishing, 1982), p. 37 (from *Saturday Evening Post*, October 1981).

6. "The Girl Who Almost Killed Ford," *Time*, September 15, 1975, p. 17.

7. "Fromme's Fate," *Time*, December 8, 1975, p. 15.

8. "Sara Jane Moore," *Washington Post*, September 24, 1975, p. A12.

9. "Miss Moore Given a Life Term," *New York Times*, January 16, 1976, p. 1.

10. "Hinckley Stalked Jodie at Yale," *New York Daily News*, May 26, 1982, p. 3.

Chapter IV

1. Ralph Wiley, "Then All the Joy Turned to Sorrow," *Sports Illustrated*, November 22, 1982, p. 28.

2. Ibid, p. 32.

3. *Time*, November 29, 1982, p. 86.

4. "Brain Beating Is No Sport," *New York Times*, November 17, 1982, p. A34.

5. Ronald J. Ross et al., "Boxers, Computed Tomography, EEG and Neurological Evaluation," *Journal of the American Medical Association*, January 14, 1983, p. 211.

6. *New York Times*, October 26, 1982, p. C1.

7. "Hockey: Fastest, Roughest Team Game in This Country," *Medical Tribune*, January 6, 1965.

8. Steve Marantz, "Hysterics Have Boxing on the Ropes," *Boston Globe*, November 16, 1982, p. 63.

9. *New York Times,* letter to the editor, December 20, 1982, p. 18.

10. "The Psychology of Team Competition," paper presented at the annual meeting of the American Psychiatric Association, Atlantic City, May 12, 1966.

11. *Time,* November 29, 1982, p. 86.

12. "If Players Fight, Fans Follow," *New York Times,* January 13, 1980, p. 2S.

13. Ibid.

14. Bill Gilbert and Lisa Twyman, "Violence: Out of Hand in the Stands," *Sports Illustrated,* p. 74.

CHAPTER V

1. *Time,* January 3, 1983, p. 78.

2. Wendy Fox, "3000 Join March in Outrage Over Rape," *Boston Globe,* March 15, 1983, p. 25.

3. Helen E. Fisher, *The Sex Contract* (New York: William Morrow, 1982), p. 222.

4. A. Rosenfeld, "When Women Rape Men," *Omni,* p. 194; Mary Baldeschwiler, "Rape Prevention Requires Curbing Social Premium on Aggression," *Texas Times,* September 1980, p. 2.

5. C. A. Martin, M. C. Warfield, and G. R. Braen, "Physicians' Management of the Psychological Aspects of Rape," *Journal of the American Medical Association,* January 28, 1983, pp. 501–503.

6. Gary McMillan, "Understanding Gang Rape Patterns," *Boston Globe,* April 11, 1983, p. 1.

7. Kurt Weiss and Sandra Borges, "Victimology and Rape," in *Rape Victimology,* edited by Leroy Schultz (Springfield, Ill.: Charles C. Thomas, 1975) (originally in *Issues of Criminology,* Vol. 8, No. 2, [Fall 1973], pp. 71–115).

8. *Encyclopedia of Human Behavior,* Vol. 2 (New York: Doubleday), p. 1093.

9. Frank Faso and Stuart Marques, "Find Record Executive Guilty of Rape," *New York Daily News.*

10. Robert K. Ressler, Ann Wolbert Burgess, and John E. Douglas, "Rape and Rape-Murder: One Offender and Twelve Victims," *American Journal of Psychiatry,* January 1983, p. 36.

11. C. A. Martin, M. C. Warfield, and G. R. Braen, "Physicians' Management of the Psychological Aspects of Rape," January 28, 1983, p. 503.

Chapter VI

1. J. F. Arnold, "Short-Circuiting Abusive Behavior," *Consultant,* July 1983, p. 204.

2. Bella English and Don Singleton, "Violence Links to Job Loss," *New York Daily News,* May 11, 1983, p. 25.

3. "Nab Dad in Aerial Abuse," *New York Daily News,* February 5, 1983, p. 2.

4. "Abuse of Adolescents Held Underreported," *Pediatric News,* December 1980, p. 15.

5. News release, University of Texas at Austin, March 3, 1980.

6. News release, American Academy of Pediatrics, November 10, 1982.

7. *Focus,* Harvard Medical Area, February 17, 1983, p. 1.

8. News release, Children's Hospital Medical Center, Boston, April 20, 1983.

9. "Violence Gives Nation Deeper Scars," *MGH News,* December 1980.

10. News release, Children's Hospital Medical Center, Boston, April 20, 1983.

11. Richard K. Goldstein and Ann W. Page, "Battered Wife Syndrome: Overview of Dynamics and Treatment," *American Journal of Psychiatry,* August 1981, pp. 1036–1043.

12. *APA Monitor,* American Psychological Association, April 1983, p. 24.

13. News release, American Psychological Association, April 1983.

14. Paper presented at American Orthopsychiatric Association meeting, Boston, April 4–8, 1983.

CHAPTER VII

1. F. Schmalleger, "World of the Career Criminal," *Human Nature,* March 1, 1979, p. 55.

2. Project Fisherman, "The Crime of Prison," Boston.

3. Stanley Penn, "Brothers in Blood," *Wall Street Journal,* May 11, 1983, pp. 1, 24.

4. Timothy Leland, "A Crisis in U.S. Prisons," *Boston Globe,* October 13, 1983, p. 45.

5. "Non-Jail Penalties under Study by U.S.," *New York Times.*

6. F. Schmalleger, "World of the Career Criminal," *Human Nature,* March 1, 1979, p. 52.

7. Project Fisherman, "The Crime of Prison," Boston.

CHAPTER VIII

1. "Why the Justice System Fails," *Time,* March 23, 1981, p. 20.

2. Margaret Gentry, "Try Violent Juveniles in Adult Courts," *Boston Herald-American,* October 1978, p. 1.

3. William Raspberry, "When a Criminal Is Beyond Human," *Boston Globe,* October 25, 1982, p. 10.

4. *Encyclopedia of Religion and Ethics,* Vol. IV (New York: Charles Scribner's Sons, 1961), p. 248.

5. Edward J. Sachar, "Behavioral Science and Criminal Law," *Scientific American,* November 1963, p. 41.

6. "The Burger Gauntlet," *Christian Science Monitor,* February 11, 1981, p. 22.

7. John Langone, "Fearful Days in Atlanta," *Discover,* April 1981, p. 47.

8. Ibid, p. 48.

9. "Almost 25 Percent of Homicides in City Tied to Drugs," *New York Times,* January 1983, p. B1.

10. Leonard Berkowitz, "How Guns Control Us," *Psychology Today,* June 1981, p. 12.

11. Ibid.

12. "Why John Hinckley Had a Gun," *New York Times,* February 2, 1983, p. 22.

13. "The Duel over Gun Control," *Time,* March 23, 1981, p. 25.

14. Adam Smith, "Guns and the American Way," *San Francisco Chronicle,* April 4, 1981, p. 32 (originally in *Esquire,* April 1981).

15. "Crimes of Violence," U.S. Government Staff Report, 1969, pp. 925–926.

16. Paper presented at the meeting of the American Association for the Advancement of Science, Washington, D.C., December 29, 1972.

17. Ibid.

18. Ibid.

19. Ibid.

20. *Clinical Psychiatry News,* July 1982, p. 10.

INDEX